The Money Within: Why We Think, Feel, and Behave Our Way Into Wealth or Struggle

Elias Morgan

THE MONEY WITHIN: WHY WE THINK, FEEL, AND BEHAVE OUR WAY INTO WEALTH OR STRUGGLE

First edition. August 1, 2025.

Copyright © 2025 Elias Morgan.

Written by Elias Morgan.

Preface

When I first began contemplating this book, I found myself returning again and again to a deceptively simple question: why, despite all the information at our fingertips, do so many of us struggle to translate financial knowledge into sustainable well-being? In an era when every new app promises to reveal the optimal savings rate, every financial blog purports to unlock the perfect investment formula, and every influencer on social media appears to have cracked the code to instant wealth, we are paradoxically more anxious, more uncertain, and more disconnected from our own money lives than at any point in history. This contradiction haunted me: how could a society that prides itself on mastery of data, logic, and technological prowess remain so vulnerable to the most basic obstacles—our own emotions, our ingrained habits, and the myths we tell ourselves about what money is supposed to deliver?

I spent the better part of a decade exploring that question from every angle, as a personal finance writer, as an interviewer of financial experts, and, perhaps most importantly, as a fellow human being far too prone to the same emotional misfires that plague nearly everyone who tries to manage money. I read study after study in behavioral economics, psychology, and neuroscience, learning how our brains misinterpret risk, how they fall prey to shortcuts that once kept our ancestors alive but now lead us to panic-sell or chase the latest fad, and how deeply our earliest memories of scarcity or abundance continue to color our financial choices decades later. I immersed myself in biographies of legendary investors and entrepreneurs, searching for patterns of thought and behavior that transcended the particulars of time or market cycle.

And I gathered countless stories—of people who lost fortunes by acting too rashly, of those who quietly built wealth by embracing patience, of individuals who found freedoms in defining "enough" for themselves, and of families who transformed generational trauma not by seeking more, but by healing the hidden wounds that triggered endless striving.

Yet, after all that research and all those conversations, I remained struck by how little of that insight ever fully sank in, even for the most diligent readers. My inbox filled with emails from people who "knew better" but could not behave better—who described in precise detail the irrational trap they had fallen into, yet found themselves powerless to choose differently in the moment when fear or desire demanded action. It became clear that the missing link in most financial education was never the absence of information, but the lack of a clear pathway from insight to enduring change. We can learn the correct theory of compounding interest; we can recite the principles of diversification until we're blue in the face; we can even simulate crisis scenarios with spreadsheets and worst-case projections. But when the real test arrives—when the market tumbles, when our emotions surge, when life throws an unexpected curveball— knowledge alone is a fragile shield.

That insight led me to reorient this book not around which investments to buy, which products to choose, or even which formulas to memorize, but rather around the one variable that consistently shapes every outcome: human behavior. If your actions determine whether you save or spend, whether you hold or sell, whether you give away or accumulate, and if habitual patterns of thought and emotion drive those actions far more reliably than any spreadsheet, then behavior must be the true asset. It follows that the central work of anyone who wants to do well with money is not the relentless hunt for a better yield or the perfect timing of market cycles, but the patient, courageous practice of shaping mindsets, rituals, and responses so that every financial decision—even the smallest spending choice or the most intimidating downturn— becomes an opportunity for consistency, clarity, and alignment with deeper values.

You will not find here exhaustive tables of asset allocations, detailed forecasts of emerging market sectors, or bullet-proof timing models. Instead, you will find guided reflections, long-form narratives, and practical frameworks designed to help you:

- **Understand the hidden forces** that hijack your choices—biases, triggers, and emotional shortcuts inherited from evolution and childhood alike;

- **Cultivate self-awareness** by observing and recording your real-time reactions to financial events, so you can design guardrails that protect you from your own worst impulses;

- **Build behavioral systems**—habits, automations, routines—that reduce reliance on willpower and turn good intentions into default actions;

- **Embrace long-term thinking** in a world built on instant feedback, so that the slow, steady power of compounding becomes an ally rather than an abstract concept;

- **Define "enough" on your own terms**, rather than by the shifting standards of comparison that keep most people trapped on a treadmill of perpetual dissatisfaction;

- **Develop emotional resilience** so you can stay calm in a downturn, know when to stand fast, and when to adapt, without letting fear or greed dictate your moves;

- **Choose contentment and generosity** as strategic advantages—because needing less of what the world sells frees you to invest more of what you truly value.

These ideas may seem nothing more than the familiar refrains of behavioral finance, but they only truly take hold when you live them, repeatedly and in the face of real discomfort. That is why each chapter of this book blends deeper context with actionable exercises and reflective prompts, designed not just to inform your mind but to engage your day-to-day practice. The most profound learning often happens not in a single "aha" moment, but in the quiet discipline of showing up—checking your journal, reviewing your spending, pausing before a rash decision, automating a new habit, or simply taking a breath when you feel the tug of an unhelpful impulse.

My hope is that this book will serve as a companion on that journey. If you bring a willingness to examine your own story—past wounds, learned biases, and habitual reactions—and if you commit to applying even a fraction of these insights through small acts of intention, you will find that the most reliable route to financial well-being lies not in chasing the next big win, but in cultivating the sturdiness of character that carries you through each twist and turn. Over time, the accumulation of those behaviors will outstrip any technical strategy you might have devised in isolation.

To those who pick up this book seeking a quick fix or a guaranteed formula, I offer this challenge: be prepared to invest in yourself with the same seriousness you would invest your capital. Treat your emotional patterns, your mental models, and your daily habits as the raw materials of wealth creation. Realize that the greatest financial risk is to believe that you can outsmart your own nature, and that the greatest financial opportunity is to learn to work with it, rather than against it.

Finally, know that you are not alone on this path. Every reader of these pages is wrestling with the tension between aspiration and contentment, between fear and faith, between impulse and discipline. We are all human, and our relationship with money is one of life's most potent mirrors, revealing both our shadows and our strengths. May this book help you see your own reflection more clearly, guide you to uncover the tools you already possess, and inspire you to shape your behavior in ways that serve not only your balance sheet, but the life you truly want to build.

Here's to the real asset—*you*—and to the choices you will make today, tomorrow, and in the years to come, that compound into a future of genuine abundance, security, and peace.

Introduction

When we think about writing a book on money—on investing, budgeting, or building lasting wealth—it is easy to fall into familiar patterns of instruction: here is the formula for compound interest, here are the asset classes you should diversify into, here is the spreadsheet template you ought to follow. The logic is so neatly packaged that it gives us a sense of control over a subject that, in reality, feels anything but controllable: markets crash, economies shift, new technologies disrupt, and personal circumstances change overnight. Yet for all the technical acuity available in today's financial media, what it rarely addresses is the single most powerful variable in every money story: human behavior.

This book exists to correct that imbalance. Its purpose is not merely to illuminate which investments hold promise or which budgeting strategies produce numerical gains. Rather, it invites you to undertake a deeper journey: a journey into the landscape of your own mind, into the habits and impulses that shape every decision you make with money, and into the ways in which your relationship with wealth extends far beyond dollar amounts to touch on identity, purpose, and well-being. If you are looking for a quick checklist or a get-rich-quick blueprint, you will not find it here. Instead, you will find a framework for cultivating the self-awareness, resilience, and long-term thinking that true financial freedom demands.

Why begin here—with behavior, not balance sheets? Because knowledge, research has shown, matters far less than we like to admit once the rubber meets the road. You can read every book ever written on investing, attend every seminar on personal finance, memorize every formula for risk-adjusted returns— and still make disastrous choices if you become fearful in a downturn, greedy in a rally, or impatient when progress moves slowly. Conversely, you can lack sophisticated models or advanced degrees, but if you have developed the habits of saving regularly, investing patiently, and thinking long term, you will almost certainly build more wealth than your overeducated, under-disciplined peers.

The chapters that follow each explore a different dimension of this central insight. We begin by considering the ways our brains are wired for immediate threats and short-term rewards, and how this evolutionary inheritance—once a survival advantage—now betrays us in decisions about saving, investing, and spending. We examine the cognitive biases that cause us to chase returns at the wrong moment and abandon sound strategies when the pain of temporary loss feels too real. We pause to reflect on the moving goalposts of satisfaction, wondering why the finish line never arrives, and discover the profound peace that comes from defining "enough" on our own terms. We look at the cost of comparing ourselves to others, and learn how contentment can become a competitive advantage when most people remain entrapped in endless comparison. We uncover the subtle ways in which ego, pride, and fear of shame shape our sense of risk, and how a humble, values-driven approach can anchor us in decisions we can live with—no matter what the market does.

Throughout this exploration, you will be invited to ask yourself frank, sometimes uncomfortable questions: What emotions arise when I think about money? Where did those feelings come from? Which financial habits serve me, and which subvert my goals? What stories have I inherited—about wealth, about success, about scarcity—that I have never examined? How often do I let headlines and trends guide my choices, rather than the quiet, consistent work of my own plan? The answers to these questions will not arrive in the form of definitive pronouncements, but as seeds of insight you will cultivate through reflection, journaling, and the practical exercises sprinkled throughout each chapter.

One of the most liberating discoveries you will make is that you need not be perfect. Behavior change rarely follows a straight line. You will stumble. You will revert to old patterns. You will experience days when panic rises and nights when doubt keeps you awake. But each slip is not a failure; it is information. It is an opportunity to learn more about how your mind works, and to refine the guardrails that protect you from your own worst impulses. Over time, as you build small victories—automating core behaviors, learning to pause before reacting, aligning your spending with your values, and embracing the long game

—you will find that change becomes easier, because it is rooted not in fleeting motivation, but in systems and identity.

Software and apps can help. Financial products can simplify tasks. Advisors can offer guidance. But no third party can feel your emotions or choose for you in the hours when stakes feel highest. You, and only you, inhabit the seat of every decision: whether to contribute to retirement before you pay that credit card bill, whether to talk honestly with a partner about money, whether to say no to an impulse purchase that carries hidden regret, whether to rebalance your portfolio when the headlines scream to sell. Your behavior

—day in, day out—is the engine of your financial life.

That is why this book—and this introduction—begins with you rather than with the market. It is a call to invest in your own capacity: your emotional resilience, your long-term perspective, your self-awareness, and your daily habits. Think of it as the most important portfolio you will ever manage. Every chapter will help you deposit into that portfolio, not by adding another line to your spreadsheet, but by shortening the distance between knowing what to do and actually doing it—especially when circumstances feel uncertain, when emotions surge, or when the siren call of quick fixes beckons.

You may wonder: can behavior really matter that much? I assure you it can—because while the world changes around you, and while no one can predict interest rates or geopolitical events with certainty, your own patterns of action offer the only domain in which you can exert near-complete control. By sculpting your own habits, training your emotional responses, and sharpening your long-horizon focus, you erect a foundation so robust that it will endure crises, opportunities, and everything in between.

This doesn't mean you become insensitive to the environment. It does not mean ignoring new developments or declining to adjust your strategy when the underlying facts change. Instead, it means responding from a place of clarity rather than reactivity. When you have built a strong behavioral core, you can update your approach with precision—knowing which metrics matter, which noise to ignore, and which decisions to double down on because they align with your deepest goals.

Above all, this book champions a perspective of agency. You are not a passive observer of market cycles or personal circumstances. You are the architect of your own experience. Each financial decision—no matter how small—reflects a choice about who you are and who you will become. By shifting the spotlight from external tactics to internal terrain, you reclaim the power to shape your financial—and, by extension, your personal—destiny.

The journey ahead is not easy. It requires candor, humility, and sustained effort. It asks you to question assumptions, to confront uncomfortable truths, and to build resilience through trial and reflection. But it also promises a payoff far beyond numbers: a sense of mastery over your choices, a release from the tyranny of fleeting impulses, and a grounded confidence that whatever the external world brings, you will meet it with equanimity and free will.

If you are prepared to do that work—if you are willing to go beyond the comfort of formulas and into the deeper territory of your own mind—then you are ready to begin. Turn the page, and let us explore how behavior, not simply knowledge, becomes the true asset in the pursuit of lasting financial well-being.

Chapter 1: It's Not What You Know—It's What You Do

There is an unspoken assumption, deeply embedded in how we approach money, success, and life decisions, that knowledge alone is the key to mastery—that if we simply acquire the right information, the right degrees, the right spreadsheet formulas or market predictions, then everything else will fall effortlessly into place. It is an appealing idea, of course, especially in a world that so heavily rewards the appearance of intellect, the accumulation of credentials, and the ability to sound like you know what you're talking about. But in the real world—in the one where rent is due, where market crashes don't knock first, and where decisions are made not in labs but in living rooms—that idea begins to fall apart.

Because the uncomfortable truth is this: doing well with money has far less to do with how much you know and far more to do with how you behave when knowledge meets pressure, uncertainty, or desire.

You don't need to be a financial genius to build wealth. In fact, history is full of highly educated, mathematically brilliant people who made catastrophic financial choices, not because they lacked information, but because they lacked behavioral control. They knew better—and yet they did not do better. They could explain the mechanics of inflation or diversification to you in perfect detail, and yet when fear or ego whispered into their ears, all of that knowledge dissolved into dust. Why? Because knowledge is static. It sits on shelves, in courses, in files, waiting to be used. Behavior, on the other hand, is dynamic. It shows up in action, under pressure, in moments when you're alone with your impulses, and no amount of intelligence can replace emotional discipline when it matters most.

We are not rational creatures who occasionally feel; we are emotional creatures who sometimes reason, and this distinction is not just philosophical—it's profoundly financial. Money touches everything: our sense of safety, our identity, our relationships, our future, and our past. It's not just numbers in an account; it's memory, it's hope, it's fear, it's control. And because money is tangled up with emotion, our decisions about it are often far less logical than we'd like to admit. You can know that you should invest long-term and not touch your portfolio, but when you see red numbers flashing and the market is spiraling, that knowledge might vanish in the face of panic. You can understand debt ratios and compound interest, but still find yourself reaching for a credit card when loneliness, envy, or stress knocks on your door.

Financial behavior is rarely just about the money. It is a reflection of deeper patterns—of how we delay gratification, how we respond to fear, how we handle boredom, how we relate to success and failure. That's why teaching personal finance purely as a numbers game is like teaching someone how to swim by showing them diagrams of a pool. Eventually, they have to get into the water. And when they do, what matters most is not what they've memorized—it's how they move when the current shifts, how they breathe when panic rises, how they adapt when the depth surprises them. The same is true with money.

Consider this: two people can receive the exact same financial advice—same strategy, same data, same timing—and one of them will thrive while the other self-destructs. Why? Because financial success is personal. It's not built in a vacuum. It's built in the context of personality, upbringing, culture, past trauma, and emotional temperament. One person may fear risk because they grew up watching their parents lose everything in a recession. Another may chase risk because they're trying to prove they're nothing like the cautious family they grew up in. Knowledge may tell both of them the same thing, but their actions will diverge wildly. Behavior, in this way, is the real differentiator.

And yet, in school, we are rarely taught this. We are taught to balance budgets, calculate returns, and perhaps memorize a few economic principles. But we are not taught how to identify our money stories, how to pause before making an impulsive purchase, how to examine our emotional triggers, or how to stay the course when everyone else is panicking. No textbook teaches you how to resist the temptation to upgrade your lifestyle the moment your income increases. No formula explains how to sit in discomfort instead of numbing it with spending. These are emotional skills, psychological muscles—and most people never train them.

The irony is that the more intelligent you are, the more likely you are to overestimate your ability to control your behavior. Intelligence can trick you into believing you're immune to human tendencies— pride, greed, denial, envy—when in reality, you might just be better at rationalizing them. The person who can fluently explain market cycles might also be the person who makes the biggest mistakes during a downturn, not because they don't know what's happening, but because they believe they can outsmart it. Intelligence without humility can be dangerous. Knowledge without behavioral discipline can be destructive.

In contrast, someone with average intelligence but a strong understanding of their emotional patterns— someone who knows their own triggers, who sets up systems to protect themselves from impulsive behavior, who understands that patience is more powerful than prediction—can build lasting wealth. Not because they have all the answers, but because they consistently follow simple principles. They don't try to be brilliant. They try to be consistent. And that makes all the difference.

We live in a culture that glorifies complexity. Complex advice, complex tools, complex strategies. But most of personal finance comes down to very simple behavior: live below your means, save consistently, invest with patience, avoid unnecessary risk, and don't panic when things go wrong. These principles are simple

—but not easy. Why? Because they ask us to do something far more difficult than math: they ask us to manage ourselves.

And self-management is one of the most undervalued skills in the financial world. It doesn't look impressive on paper. It won't land you a job at a hedge fund. But it will help you sleep at night. It will help you build slowly and avoid collapse. It will help you say no when everyone else is saying yes. And over time, it will help you build something more meaningful than a high return: it will help you build peace.

This chapter is about shifting the focus—from what you know to how you act. From intellectual mastery to behavioral resilience. From facts and formulas to emotions and choices. In the pages that follow, we will explore five core insights that challenge the traditional narrative of money as purely a mathematical field and instead place human behavior at the very center of financial success. You'll see why being smart is not enough, why personal history can override good advice, why decision-making under pressure often defies logic, and why consistent behavior beats perfect strategy in the long run.

The goal of this chapter is not to make you feel like you're doing money wrong. It's to show you that you're not alone—that most of us struggle not because we're ignorant, but because we're human. And if we can begin to understand our own patterns, to build systems that account for our humanity instead of pretending we're machines, then we can start to make better decisions—not just smarter ones, but braver ones, kinder ones, and ultimately, more sustainable ones.

Because doing well with money isn't about being perfect. It's about being aware. It's about recognizing that every financial decision is also an emotional decision, a behavioral decision, a human decision. And if you can get better at understanding yourself, then you can get better at everything else.

The Illusion of Financial Intelligence

There is something undeniably seductive about intelligence—particularly the kind that comes dressed in numbers, projections, financial charts, and economic jargon that sounds too sophisticated to question. We live in a world where smartness is often mistaken for wisdom, where financial acumen is measured by how confidently one can speak about market trends or portfolio diversification, and where those who talk in confident tones about "leveraging assets" or "beating the index" are assumed to be ahead of the curve. But beneath that surface—beneath the spreadsheets, the confident forecasts, the polished terminology—lurks a persistent truth that too few are willing to admit: being financially intelligent is not the same as being financially wise, and the appearance of knowledge often conceals the absence of behavioral strength.

We see it everywhere—people with elite degrees in economics or finance who make catastrophic personal financial decisions, hedge fund managers who lose fortunes despite their brilliance, high-income professionals who live in quiet desperation under mountains of debt. These are not outliers; they are reminders. Reminders that financial outcomes are not always correlated with IQ, that understanding the mechanics of money is not the same as managing it well, and that the illusion of financial intelligence can be far more dangerous than ignorance itself—because it comes with overconfidence, and overconfidence is the seed from which many financial failures grow.

In fact, one of the most paradoxical realities of modern finance is that the more intellectually capable a person is, the more prone they might be to assuming they are immune to error. They may believe they are too smart to be influenced by emotion, too informed to be swayed by trends, too rational to fall for cognitive biases. But that belief itself becomes the trap. Because the moment you think you are above human behavior, you become even more vulnerable to its effects—only now, you have the added danger of not noticing when it happens. This is the illusion of financial intelligence: the false sense that knowledge alone can protect you from poor choices, when in fact, knowledge without humility and self-awareness is often just a well-dressed version of denial.

The truth is that finance—particularly personal finance—is not an IQ game. It is a behavior game. It is a discipline game. It is a self-knowledge game. And these are not skills that can be taught in a traditional academic environment. You don't learn self-control from a textbook. You don't learn delayed gratification from a TED Talk. You don't build financial resilience by memorizing the definition of inflation. These are lived traits—earned through experience, cultivated through failure, and tested in moments when emotions are louder than reason.

And so the person who is most successful with money is often not the one who knows the most—but the one who knows themselves the best. The one who understands their weaknesses and designs systems to protect against them. The one who isn't trying to outsmart the market but is trying to outlast it. The one who doesn't chase returns but builds habits. The one who isn't seduced by complexity but trusts simplicity, because simplicity is harder to stray from when things get hard.

It's also important to recognize that many of the financial mistakes people make are not due to a lack of understanding, but due to a lapse in behavior. Overspending isn't usually a miscalculation—it's an emotional response to stress, boredom, loneliness, or comparison. Selling during a market dip isn't necessarily a failure of logic—it's a failure of nerve in the face of uncertainty. Taking on too much debt isn't a blind mistake—it's often a response to the psychological need to feel adequate, accomplished, or secure. And no amount of intelligence can compensate for unacknowledged emotional needs that drive these behaviors.

But because we live in a society that values intellect so highly, we often overestimate the protective power of knowledge. We think, "If only I knew more, I'd make better decisions." And sometimes that's true. But more often, the truth is this: you don't need more knowledge—you need more awareness, more restraint, more self-trust, and more systems that prevent your worst impulses from hijacking your best intentions.

Financial media, too, plays a role in sustaining this illusion. We are constantly bombarded with analysis, forecasts, expert opinions, stock picks, market commentary—information designed to make us feel that the key to financial success is simply knowing the right thing at the right time. But what gets lost in all of that noise is the quieter, more enduring truth: most of the wealthiest, most financially stable people in the world didn't get there by being the smartest person in the room. They got there by doing simple things consistently, by avoiding big mistakes, by staying the course when others panicked, and by refusing to let short-term noise distract from long-term strategy.

There is a quiet humility to this kind of financial intelligence—one that doesn't announce itself with complex terminology, one that isn't obsessed with prediction, one that doesn't try to impress others with knowledge. It's the kind of intelligence that shows up in habits, in systems, in boundaries. It's the intelligence of someone who says no to things they can afford, because they know their real wealth lies in freedom. It's the intelligence of someone who doesn't care about timing the market, because they care more about time in the market. It's the intelligence of someone who doesn't need to look smart, because they care more about being secure.

That kind of intelligence is not loud. It's not flashy. It doesn't show up in headlines. But it builds something solid. Something lasting.

The illusion of financial intelligence, by contrast, is brittle. It relies on performance, on control, on the constant need to prove something to someone—often to yourself. It leads people to take on risks they don't understand, to chase status symbols that bring no real satisfaction, to follow advice that doesn't match their context, to believe they're in control when they're actually reacting unconsciously to deeper fears or unresolved emotional wounds. And because that illusion can be so powerful—because it is constantly reinforced by culture, media, and even traditional education—it takes deliberate effort to dismantle.

To dismantle it, you must be willing to ask uncomfortable questions: Am I spending to feel better, or because it makes sense? Am I investing this way because I believe in it, or because I want to seem smart? Am I chasing more because I need it, or because I'm afraid of having less than others? Am I avoiding simple strategies because I think they're beneath me, or because I fear slowing down? These are not easy questions. But they are necessary ones. Because without asking them, you may find yourself caught in the illusion—thinking that you are doing everything right, when in fact, your behavior is quietly pulling you in the wrong direction.

In the end, true financial intelligence is not about how much you know—it's about how wisely, consistently, and calmly you apply what you know. It is not about predicting the next market move—it's about preparing yourself for the fact that you won't be able to. It's not about sounding intelligent—it's about living intelligently, which often means doing less, not more; saying no, not yes; and walking away, not leaning in. It is the intelligence of restraint, of patience, of self-trust—and these are traits that will serve you far longer than any economic theory or investment hack ever could.

The illusion may be loud, but real wisdom is quiet. And if you learn to listen closely—not just to the market, but to yourself—you might just find that the most important financial insights were never about money at all. They were about behavior. About emotion. About character. And about the courage to act differently in a world that's always trying to impress.

Why Smart People Still Make Dumb Money Choices

It is one of the great paradoxes of our time—one that leaves many scratching their heads in disbelief and even more suffering quietly behind closed doors: how can people who are clearly intelligent, capable, and even professionally successful still make decisions with money that seem completely irrational, short-sighted, or downright self-destructive? How can a physician with years of rigorous training, a lawyer with a deep understanding of contracts, or a tech entrepreneur who builds complex systems from scratch, still find themselves drowning in credit card debt, overleveraged in risky investments, or chasing after the illusion of wealth through endless consumer upgrades? It's not because they're dumb. In fact, that's precisely the point—it happens *despite* their intelligence. And it happens more often than most are willing to admit.

To understand why, we need to confront a difficult truth: intelligence, as it is traditionally defined—academic performance, analytical skills, technical knowledge—does not automatically translate into sound financial behavior. The two occupy entirely different domains. One is a measure of how well you process external information; the other is a measure of how well you manage internal tension. One is cognitive; the other is emotional. One thrives on logic and structure; the other is often challenged by ambiguity, stress, and deeply rooted personal narratives. And so, while intelligence may help you understand the world, it does not necessarily help you navigate your own emotional world—especially when money is involved.

Money, after all, is not just a tool. It is a mirror. It reflects not only our goals and achievements, but also our fears, our insecurities, our desires to be seen and validated. And smart people—like all people—are not immune to these emotional currents. In fact, they are sometimes even more vulnerable, precisely because they believe they should be above them. Their intelligence becomes a shield, a way to rationalize behavior that is emotionally driven but intellectually justified after the fact. "This car isn't a splurge, it's a reward for my hard work." "This investment isn't a gamble, it's a calculated risk." "This vacation isn't reckless, it's necessary for my mental health." And so the story goes—not because the facts are always wrong, but because the emotion came first, and the justification came second.

This backward logic—making a decision emotionally and then dressing it up in rationality—is incredibly common, and it's not just a flaw in smart people; it's a universal human tendency. The difference is that intelligent individuals are often more skilled at constructing convincing narratives. They're better at making their irrational behavior *sound* rational. They know how to find the article, the chart, the expert opinion that supports what they've already decided to do. And in doing so, they create a kind of intellectual echo chamber where their choices are never challenged—only reinforced.

Add to this the fact that smart people are often rewarded in life for taking risks. In academic or professional environments, boldness and innovation are praised. Thinking differently is encouraged. Questioning the status quo is considered a sign of genius. But the financial world plays by different rules. While innovation can lead to breakthrough wealth, more often than not, consistency and restraint lead to stability. And those traits—restraint, repetition, patience—are rarely glamorous. They don't feel exciting. They don't win applause. And so, a highly intelligent person who thrives on challenge and novelty may find the slow, steady path of smart financial behavior unbearably boring. They want to optimize, to maximize, to outperform—not realizing that such impulses, left unchecked, can lead to overtrading, overinvesting, or overextending.

In some cases, intelligence also breeds overconfidence. When someone is used to being the smartest person in the room, they may begin to assume they can outsmart not only others, but also systems—systems like the market, the tax code, or even human nature itself. They may believe they can time the market because they timed their startup perfectly. They may believe they can take on high-interest debt because they assume their income will always rise to meet it. They may believe they are the exception to the rule, the one who will succeed where others failed. And sometimes, they do. But more often, the overconfidence becomes a blind spot, and when things go wrong—as they inevitably do—they find themselves unprepared for the consequences, because they never really believed those consequences applied to them in the first place.

There is also another layer to consider—one that rarely gets mentioned in financial conversations but plays an enormous role in shaping behavior: identity. For many smart, successful people, their sense of self is deeply tied to their ability to appear competent, accomplished, and in control. Financial mistakes don't just feel like setbacks—they feel like personal failures, evidence that maybe they aren't as smart as they appear. And that fear can lead to denial, to secrecy, to the inability to ask for help or admit they're struggling. They may double down on bad decisions rather than confront them, because to backtrack would mean exposing a crack in the armor they've spent their whole lives building. And so they suffer silently, locked in a cycle of pride and avoidance, until the financial damage becomes too big to ignore.

The pressure to maintain appearances—especially in a world dominated by social media and performative success—only makes this worse. When you're smart, people expect you to have it all figured out. They expect you to live in the right neighborhood, drive the right car, vacation in the right places. And sometimes, keeping up with those expectations becomes a full-time job—one that drains both money and mental energy. The person who appears wealthy may, in fact, be leveraged to the hilt. The person who appears calm and competent may be lying awake at night, wondering how they'll pay the bills. But because they're smart—because they're used to projecting competence—they keep the mask on, even when the cost of wearing it grows heavier by the day.

The truth is that being smart is not enough. Not with money. Not in a world where temptation is everywhere, where access to credit is easier than ever, where financial products are increasingly complex and emotionally seductive, and where the pressure to perform is relentless. To navigate this world successfully, you need more than intelligence. You need insight. You need emotional literacy. You need self-control, self-awareness, and the humility to recognize that being smart doesn't make you immune—it just gives you more sophisticated ways to justify your mistakes.

And here is the most hopeful part: financial behavior can be learned. Not in the traditional sense—not by memorizing more facts or mastering more terminology—but by observing your patterns, reflecting on your choices, and building systems that make good behavior easier and bad behavior harder. It means recognizing when your intelligence is serving you, and when it's working against you. It means learning to pause before reacting, to question your own assumptions, to ask not just "Is this smart?" but "Is this wise, given who I am, where I am, and what I actually value?"

Because wisdom is not about outsmarting others—it's about outsmarting your own ego. It's about having the courage to admit when you're wrong, the patience to stick with what works, and the clarity to choose long-term peace over short-term prestige. And none of that requires a genius-level IQ. It requires something far rarer: self-honesty.

So if you've ever found yourself wondering why you, or someone you admire, keeps making money choices that don't align with what they know—don't assume the problem is intelligence. In most cases, it's not. It's emotion. It's pressure. It's pride. And until those forces are understood and addressed, even the smartest minds will keep falling into the same traps, again and again.

Smart people make dumb money choices not because they're flawed, but because they're human. And the path to better choices begins not with more knowledge—but with deeper self-awareness.

1.3 Knowing Isn't Doing – The Behavior Gap

There is a quiet, persistent illusion that deceives even the most well-meaning among us—one that whispers that once we understand something, we have mastered it, that the moment we grasp the concept intellectually, the transformation is complete. In personal development, it shows up in the form of quotes shared but not lived; in fitness, it shows up as plans made but not executed; and in finance, it shows up with startling frequency as knowledge unacted upon—books read, podcasts listened to, courses completed

—yet habits unchanged, savings stagnant, and peace of mind as elusive as ever. This is the great divide that lives at the heart of nearly every financial struggle: the gap between knowing and doing.

It is easy to assume that people who are financially unstable simply don't know better—that if they only understood budgeting, investing, or saving, they would immediately make better choices. But in reality, most people already *do* know what they should be doing. They know they should spend less than they earn. They know they should save for the future. They know credit card debt is costly and impulsive purchases rarely bring lasting joy. And yet, they do the opposite—not because they're ignorant, but because information alone is not enough to change behavior. Knowledge is passive; behavior is active. And the bridge between the two is far longer and more fragile than most are willing to admit.

This divide—the behavior gap—is not a flaw in intelligence, but a reflection of how deeply human beings are shaped by emotion, environment, and habit. We may read about compound interest and feel inspired, but when the urge for a dopamine hit rises on a Friday night, that abstract concept loses its power. We may understand the importance of long-term investing, but when headlines scream of recessions and crashes, logic gives way to panic. We may know the math behind buying a used car over a new one, but the pull of prestige, of looking successful in front of others, often overrides the data. And so, over and over, we find ourselves caught in the same cycle—not because we don't know better, but because the knowing never turned into doing.

Behavior is messy, especially when money is involved, because money is never just about math—it is about identity, emotion, memory, and fear. It is about safety and self-worth. It is about how we see ourselves and how we want others to see us. And these forces operate not in spreadsheets but in the subconscious, in the quiet spaces where logic can't always reach. That is why financial progress requires more than education; it requires transformation. It requires designing your life in a way that supports good behavior even when motivation is low, when fear is high, or when the path forward isn't perfectly clear.

Take, for example, the person who binge-watches financial education videos on YouTube, subscribes to every newsletter, follows experts on social media, and feels deeply informed—yet still lives paycheck to paycheck. On paper, they are financially literate. But in practice, their behavior hasn't shifted. Why?

Because there is no accountability, no system, no emotional scaffolding to support the knowledge. They feel empowered in the moment of consumption, but when the emotional weight of daily life returns— stress, comparison, boredom, insecurity—their actions default to habit, not insight.

The behavior gap also persists because we underestimate just how powerful the environment around us is. We think we are making independent choices, but often we are merely reacting to the culture we're immersed in—one that encourages consumption, glorifies urgency, and rewards appearance over substance. You might know you should save for retirement, but you're surrounded by peers who upgrade their lifestyle every time they get a raise. You might understand the long-term benefits of index investing, but your social media feed is full of people bragging about crypto flips and trading wins. In such an environment, knowledge becomes background noise, drowned out by louder messages that trigger emotion and short-term thinking.

To close the behavior gap, then, we must stop pretending that financial success is a matter of willpower or knowledge alone. We must instead turn toward the architecture of our behavior—toward the systems and boundaries that make good decisions easier and bad ones harder. That means automating savings so you don't have to rely on discipline. It means creating spending rules so you don't have to debate every purchase. It means using friction to your advantage—making impulsive actions inconvenient and thoughtful actions seamless.

But beyond systems, closing the gap also requires confronting your own narrative—your internal story about money, success, worth, and fear. Because if you carry a belief that you're not "good with money," you'll find ways to sabotage your efforts, even when you know what to do. If you believe that wealth is for "other people," you'll reject opportunities to grow. If you associate saving with deprivation, you'll avoid it even when it's logical. The stories we carry shape the actions we take—or avoid. And no amount of knowledge can override a subconscious belief you haven't named and dismantled.

Perhaps this is the most humbling truth of all: behavior is not always rational, and it does not always follow knowledge. In fact, human behavior is often defensive, emotional, and contradictory. You can want two opposing things at once. You can know better and still do worse. And that doesn't make you broken— it makes you human. The challenge, then, is not to become perfectly rational, but to become aware of your irrationality and to build a life that makes room for it. A life where discipline is supported by design, where you don't have to be constantly strong, just consistently protected from your own worst impulses.

There's a reason why athletes practice drills even when they know the game. There's a reason why pilots use checklists even after thousands of hours of flight. It's because knowledge, under pressure, is unreliable. It's because when stakes are high, your brain defaults not to logic, but to habit. And this is true in money, too. The behavior gap is not closed by knowing more, but by practicing better. By making the right choice easier than the wrong one. By creating defaults that work in your favor. By recognizing that good behavior is not about strength—it's about strategy.

And this strategy must be personal. It must take into account your unique triggers, your history, your environment. Because the reason *you* aren't saving might be different from the reason *someone else* isn't saving. The reason you overspend might be rooted in emotional wounds or cultural expectations that no budgeting app can touch. So the question is not "Why don't I do what I know?" The question is "What emotional or situational barrier is preventing action, and how can I remove it or work around it?"

Closing the behavior gap is not glamorous work. It doesn't make headlines. It doesn't make you feel instantly smarter. But it is where all real transformation begins. And once you start to see it—not just in yourself but in others—you begin to understand that financial outcomes are rarely about intelligence or even effort. They are about whether someone was able to align their behavior with their values consistently, quietly, and without needing external validation.

So if you've been blaming yourself for not doing what you know you should do—pause. Take a breath. Then realize that you are not failing because you lack knowledge. You are struggling because knowledge and behavior live in different rooms, and building a bridge between them takes intention, time, and compassion. The gap is real. But it is also crossable.

And the moment you stop asking "What's the right thing to do?" and start asking "How do I actually *do* the right thing in the context of my real life?"—that's the moment you begin to move. Not perfectly. But meaningfully. Not instantly. But consistently.

That's how behavior changes. That's how habits form. And ultimately, that's how lives are transformed.

The Real Classroom – Life, Not Lectures

There is something profoundly comforting about the structure of a classroom—about its linear progress, its clear objectives, its neat division between student and teacher, knowledge and ignorance, success and failure. In that carefully contained environment, we come to believe that learning is a matter of intake— that the more information we absorb, the more capable we become, and that once we've been taught something, we've truly learned it. But the real world, especially the financial world, does not operate on that kind of predictability. It does not hand out syllabi. It does not offer multiple-choice exams. And most importantly, it does not wait for you to feel "ready." It throws you into its lessons without asking your permission, often before you've learned the rules, and with consequences that extend far beyond a grade point average.

This is the fundamental misunderstanding that keeps so many people trapped in financial frustration: the belief that personal finance can be truly mastered in the classroom, that the lectures, seminars, and certifications can somehow prepare you for the deeply emotional, high-stakes, and often chaotic world in which financial decisions are actually made. But the truth is this: the real education—the kind that sticks, the kind that transforms, the kind that actually rewires how you behave—doesn't come from lectures. It comes from life.

Life teaches you in ways no textbook can. Life teaches you through the embarrassment of overdrawn accounts, through the ache of buyer's remorse, through the pit in your stomach when you realize you can't afford to fix the car you depend on to get to work. Life teaches you when you lend money to a friend out of guilt, only to be left betrayed. Life teaches you when you max out a credit card chasing a feeling, and then spend months—or years—trying to recover. These moments, painful as they are, carve lessons deeper than any lecture ever could. They force reflection. They spark growth. And most importantly, they humble you in a way that knowledge alone never will.

You can understand compound interest in theory, but it takes seeing it work—or watching it fail due to impatience—to truly respect it. You can recite the definition of opportunity cost, but until you've chosen short-term pleasure over long-term stability and lived with the aftermath, that concept remains just another academic phrase. You can know that emergencies happen, but until life surprises you with a medical bill, a job loss, or a family crisis, saving for one may still feel optional. Real understanding doesn't come from reading about other people's mistakes. It comes from making your own—and choosing to learn from them.

And yet, despite this truth, so much of financial education remains disconnected from the emotional and contextual realities of everyday life. We are taught how to calculate returns, but not how to manage envy when our friends are advancing faster than we are. We are taught how to plan for retirement, but not how to navigate the guilt of saying no to people we love in order to protect our savings. We are taught the mechanics of budgeting, but not the psychology of spending. And so we find ourselves overprepared for abstract problems, but underprepared for the lived complexity of real decisions—the kind made in moments of stress, fatigue, loneliness, or hope.

Because the truth is, most financial choices are not made with spreadsheets in front of us. They are made in conversation, in quiet moments, in reaction to unexpected events. You decide to buy something not because the math adds up, but because it makes you feel seen. You invest not because you've analyzed every risk, but because you want to believe in a better future. You borrow not because you've planned poorly, but because someone you love needs help and saying no would feel like betrayal. These decisions are emotional. They are messy. And they require a kind of intelligence that no formal education truly teaches: the intelligence of self-awareness, emotional regulation, and context.

In the real classroom of life, you are your own teacher—and your own test. You will be asked to apply what you've learned before you feel fully ready. You will be tested not just on your knowledge, but on your character. On your patience. On your ability to stay calm when everything feels uncertain. You will be challenged not once, but repeatedly, and often in new and evolving ways. You will be forced to confront not just what you believe about money, but what you believe about yourself, about your worth, about your capacity to change.

And the most powerful lessons of this classroom are not found in the successes, but in the failures. They are found in the moments when things didn't go according to plan, when your strategy broke down, when you did everything "right" and still lost. Because it is in those moments—not in lectures or certifications— that you discover your real financial philosophy. Do you panic or persist? Do you blame or adapt? Do you collapse or rebuild? These questions cannot be answered in theory. They must be lived into.

Ironically, this is why some of the most financially stable and resilient people are not the ones with the most education, but the ones with the most experience—particularly the kind of experience that humbles, sharpens, and clarifies. These people may not speak the language of finance fluently. They may not know what a P/E ratio is. But they know how to live below their means. They know how to say no to unnecessary temptation. They know how to prepare for the unexpected, how to delay gratification, how to choose peace of mind over flashy purchases. These are lessons learned not in theory, but in practice. In life. In hardship.

This is not to say that traditional financial education has no value. It does. Understanding how money works is important. But knowledge alone is not enough. What matters even more is your ability to translate that knowledge into behavior—and behavior is shaped by context, by history, by emotion. That's why someone who never finished high school can build wealth, while someone with an MBA can live in quiet debt. Because one of them learned how to manage themselves. The other only learned how to manage spreadsheets.

So if you've ever felt ashamed that you "should know better," or disappointed that you've read all the right books but still struggle to save, spend, or invest wisely—let that shame go. Because it's not about what you've learned in a classroom. It's about what you're learning in the classroom of your life. And that kind of learning is non-linear. It is imperfect. It involves detours and returns, setbacks and comebacks. It is not a curriculum you follow once—it is a lifelong process of falling forward.

Ultimately, the real classroom—the one that matters—is the one you are already in. It is the conversation you're having with your partner about money and trust. It is the decision you make at the grocery store when the cheap option feels like failure. It is the late-night worry about how to pay the bills, the unexpected windfall you're not sure how to use, the inherited belief you're trying to unlearn. It is here, in the lived reality of your own story, that the real learning happens.

And if you can begin to treat your life as the primary source of financial education—not your failures as proof of inadequacy, but as opportunities for growth; not your missteps as signs of weakness, but as signals of where to pay attention—then you will be doing something far more powerful than mastering a subject. You will be mastering yourself. And that, in the end, is the most valuable skill of all.

From Spreadsheet to Supper Table – Where Decisions Happen

There is a common misconception—often perpetuated by financial institutions, analysts, and well- intentioned experts—that our most important money decisions are made in front of glowing screens, between columns of numbers, calculated formulas, and carefully planned forecasts. In this narrative, the spreadsheet becomes a kind of sacred space, a temple of logic where every financial move is supposed to be weighed, optimized, and executed with surgical precision. But anyone who has lived outside the tidy confines of theoretical finance knows that the real decisions—the ones that shape our financial future, the ones that carry weight and consequence—are rarely made in Excel. They're made in kitchens, in bedrooms, in cars, at dinner tables, often when we're tired, emotional, distracted, or simply doing our best to hold life together.

Because real life doesn't wait for ideal conditions. It doesn't pause for market updates. It doesn't remind you to cross-reference your spending with last month's budget before the baby needs diapers, before the car breaks down, before your partner asks, with worry in their voice, whether you'll be able to pay the mortgage on time. Real life—unpredictable, unfiltered, often messy—is where our financial behavior actually unfolds. And understanding this, accepting this, is essential if we want to stop measuring our decisions against some artificial standard of rationality that ignores everything human about the way we live.

It's not that spreadsheets are useless. They have their place. They give us a framework. They help us plan, anticipate, and organize. But they don't capture the late-night impulse to "treat yourself" because you've had a terrible week. They don't factor in the emotional cost of saying no to your child when they ask for something you can't afford but wish you could. They don't reveal the subtle tension between you and your partner when your definitions of "necessity" don't align. They don't account for the embarrassment of turning down a group vacation with friends because your financial goals no longer match theirs. In the real world, money doesn't exist in isolation—it exists in relationship. And relationships are where decisions happen.

More specifically, decisions happen at the dinner table. They happen when couples quietly disagree about what qualifies as an emergency. They happen when parents feel the tug-of-war between teaching responsibility and providing comfort. They happen when families sit down to review expenses and one person is avoiding eye contact, already feeling judged. They happen in silence, in tone, in the invisible emotional landscape of the home. Because money is not just about numbers—it's about values, communication, identity, and security. And the dinner table, in all its ordinariness, becomes the arena where all of that comes into play.

This is why so many financial strategies fail—not because they're wrong, but because they're designed for people who don't exist. They assume the decision-maker is calm, rational, emotionally neutral, and fully informed. They assume there is time and space to evaluate options without pressure. But in reality, most people are making financial decisions in the midst of stress, fatigue, competing priorities, and unspoken fears. They're choosing whether to pay off a credit card or buy groceries, whether to invest in a retirement fund or fix the leaking roof, whether to take the safe job or chase a dream that might not pay. These aren't spreadsheet decisions. These are life decisions. And they require more than data—they require discernment.

They also require empathy. Empathy for ourselves and for those we make decisions with. Because so much of financial behavior is tangled up with our personal histories—how we were raised, what we lacked, what we feared, what we learned to believe about wealth, success, and survival. One person might feel anxious unless there's $10,000 in a savings account, while their partner feels confident with just enough to cover next month's bills. One might view spending on experiences as essential, while the other sees it as frivolous. And unless these differences are named and explored with compassion, financial conversations can quickly turn into conflicts—not because of the money, but because of what the money represents.

At the supper table, you're not just deciding how to budget—you're deciding how to live. You're negotiating identity. You're navigating old wounds. You're balancing today's needs against tomorrow's dreams. You're trying to stay united in a world that constantly pulls people into comparison, shame, and scarcity. And none of that is reflected in a formula. It's reflected in tone, in trust, in the willingness to pause and listen even when you disagree. It's reflected in the courage to say, "This is where I'm afraid," and the grace to respond, "I understand."

This is the terrain where financial wisdom is built—not in abstraction, but in practice. In hard conversations. In trial and error. In vulnerability. It's built when you resist the urge to lash out during a money fight and instead ask a deeper question. It's built when you acknowledge that your partner's spending habits aren't about rebellion but about the need to feel safe. It's built when you forgive yourself for past mistakes and decide, even if quietly, to try again. That's real growth. And it happens not on a page

—but around the table.

The more we can bring our full selves into these moments—the fears, the hopes, the messy truths—the more powerful our financial decisions become. Because then we're not just reacting to the numbers. We're responding to the story underneath them. We're honoring the real-life context of the choices we make.

And when we do that, we begin to create not just plans, but peace. Not just wealth, but alignment.

This is also why simplicity matters so much more than complexity. At the dinner table, you don't have time to reanalyze market trends or compare loan amortization charts. What you need is clarity. You need to know what you value. You need to agree on your goals. You need to define success not by how impressive your portfolio looks, but by how well your life reflects what matters to you. Because when that clarity exists, decisions become easier—not because they're painless, but because they're grounded in shared purpose.

And if you live alone—if your dinner table is quiet—the principle still holds. Your financial decisions are still shaped not by formulas, but by mood, by memory, by the conversations you have in your own mind. The moment you open your banking app after a long day, the moment you swipe your card out of boredom, the moment you rationalize a purchase by saying, "I deserve this"—these are not mathematical moments. They are emotional ones. And they deserve to be met with the same compassion and honesty as any conversation between two people.

So let's stop pretending that the real work of money happens in isolation, in spreadsheets, in cold analysis. Let's admit what has always been true—that the dinner table is the real financial center of most people's lives. That's where the truth comes out. That's where priorities collide. That's where transformation begins.

And if we can learn to see that table not as a place of tension but as a place of possibility, not as a battlefield but as a space for growth, then maybe—just maybe—we'll begin to treat financial conversations not as something to dread, but as something sacred. A ritual. A practice. A space where clarity, connection, and courage are built—not just for today, but for the years to come.

Chapter 2: Your Money Story Begins Early

Before you ever earned your first paycheck, before you signed your first lease, before you applied for your first credit card or opened your first bank account, your relationship with money had already begun to take shape—quietly, subtly, and often invisibly. It began not with numbers, but with moments. With overheard conversations. With anxious glances exchanged between parents. With comments made in passing, like "we can't afford that" or "money doesn't grow on trees." With the tone of voice used when bills arrived. With the feelings you absorbed, even when nothing was said at all.

Long before you had the vocabulary to explain what you were witnessing, you were internalizing messages. You were observing. You were feeling. You were making sense of what money meant—not as a tool, but as a force. And what you learned during those formative years didn't just shape your beliefs about money; it shaped your sense of what is possible, what is safe, what is expected, what is "enough." It laid the groundwork for the choices you now make, often without realizing why.

This is what we mean when we speak of a *money story*—the personal, emotional, often unconscious narrative each of us carries, shaped not by textbooks or financial advisors, but by lived experience. Your money story is not a balance sheet. It is a biography. It is a psychological imprint. And whether it is one of abundance or scarcity, control or chaos, fear or freedom, it is powerful—because it operates beneath the surface of your awareness, influencing how you think, how you feel, and ultimately, how you behave.

And like all stories, it is layered. Sometimes, your money story is told to you directly—through explicit advice, warnings, or mantras repeated by caregivers or community. Sometimes it is implied—formed through observation, through what was celebrated and what was shamed, through what was available and what was withheld. And sometimes, it is inherited—passed down through generations, carried like invisible luggage, influencing your decisions long after you've forgotten where the beliefs even came from.

Some people grow up in households where money is a constant source of tension—a presence that hangs heavy in the room, creating stress, arguments, or silence. Others grow up in homes where money is plentiful but conditional—used as a tool for control or comparison, given with strings attached, withheld as punishment. Some are raised with open conversations about budgeting and saving, while others are kept entirely in the dark, expected to "figure it out" when adulthood arrives. And these early experiences, though varied in expression, leave a mark. They become the emotional code behind your financial operating system—shaping your impulses, your fears, your tendencies.

For instance, if you grew up watching your parents panic every time the car needed repairs, you may now feel anxious about spending, even when you can afford it. If you were raised in an environment where luxury was equated with love or status, you may feel compelled to prove your worth through purchases, regardless of their actual value. If saving was praised as a virtue in your household, you may associate spending—even when necessary—with guilt. Conversely, if money was always flowing but never discussed, you may find yourself avoiding financial planning altogether, convinced that someone else will figure it out, just as they always did before.

These patterns don't always make sense on paper. They aren't necessarily logical. But they are deeply human. Because the emotional core of your money story is not about economics—it's about survival, safety, identity, and love. It's about how you were taught to feel secure, to belong, to gain approval, or to protect yourself. And those lessons—picked up in childhood, reinforced over time—become the lens through which you interpret every financial situation you face as an adult.

That's why two people with the same income, the same financial education, and the same goals can make radically different decisions. One might hoard money out of fear, the other might overspend to feel worthy. One might avoid risk because they saw what it did to their family, the other might chase risk in a desperate bid to escape the past. These aren't mistakes—they're echoes. Echoes of stories that were written long ago, in a voice that still speaks even when we think we've moved on.

Understanding this doesn't mean placing blame. It doesn't mean resenting your parents or your past. In fact, many of the people who shaped your money story were doing the best they could with what they knew. They were acting out of their own stories—their own inherited beliefs, fears, and habits. But recognizing this chain—this lineage of financial psychology—gives you something far more important than blame: it gives you *agency*. Because once you see the story, you can question it. You can rewrite it. You can choose which parts to keep, and which parts to let go.

This is the heart of financial self-awareness—not just learning how to manage money, but learning how to manage the story behind the money. It means asking questions that don't often appear in financial advice books: What did money represent in my childhood—freedom, stress, shame, power? What were the moments that shaped how I feel about wealth, poverty, giving, saving? What did I learn to fear? What did I learn to chase? What role did money play in my family's happiness—or its conflict? And how are those old patterns playing out in my current decisions?

When you begin to explore these questions, something remarkable happens. The noise begins to quiet. The shame starts to lift. You stop seeing your financial habits as personal failures and begin to recognize them as predictable responses to patterns you didn't choose—but can now change. You stop fighting yourself and start understanding yourself. And from that place of understanding, real transformation becomes possible—not through willpower or force, but through clarity.

Because clarity allows choice. And choice is where power lives.

The chapters that follow will explore the anatomy of your money story—how it forms, how it shows up in your behavior, and how you can begin to revise it into something more aligned with who you are now, not who you were then. You'll see how beliefs get encoded, how emotional associations with money are built, and how certain wounds—scarcity, shame, comparison—can quietly drive our decisions for years. But more importantly, you'll discover how to interrupt those patterns. How to become the author of your financial narrative, rather than its unconscious character.

This work isn't about perfection. It's about awareness. It's about seeing the map you've been following and asking, honestly, whether it still leads where you want to go. And if it doesn't, giving yourself permission to draw a new one.

Because your money story began early—but it doesn't have to end where it started.

The Inheritance of Belief, Not Just Wealth

When we hear the word "inheritance," our minds instinctively turn to the material—the tangible assets passed down from one generation to another: money in a trust fund, property titles, family heirlooms, perhaps a stock portfolio or a modest bank account. Inheritance, in this familiar sense, is about what is left behind in a will—what can be measured, counted, divided. But there is another kind of inheritance, far more subtle, far more pervasive, and often far more powerful than the financial kind: the inheritance of belief.

Whether we recognize it or not, every person carries within them a set of inherited beliefs about money— core assumptions absorbed through years of observation, conversation, silence, and emotion. These beliefs are not taught explicitly, and they are rarely written down. They are passed down through tone, through behavior, through unspoken rules about what is "normal," what is "right," what is "desirable," and what is "dangerous" when it comes to money. They are absorbed long before we ever have a chance to question them. And in this way, we inherit not only what our parents had, but how they thought. Not only their wealth or lack of it, but their relationship with the idea of wealth itself.

You might inherit a belief that money is scarce—that there's never quite enough, that it must be hoarded and protected, that security is an illusion and poverty is always one bad month away. Or you might inherit a belief that money is always available, always flowing, that spending freely is a sign of abundance, and that restraint signals weakness or limitation. You might inherit a belief that talking about money is rude or shameful—or that it's a tool for power and control. You might believe, without knowing where the belief came from, that wealth is corrupting, or that wanting more is greedy, or that financial struggle is virtuous and noble.

These beliefs don't enter our minds through formal instruction. No one sits us down to say, "Here is how you should feel about money." Instead, they arrive in the background of our lives, as emotional residue from the way money was handled around us. They arrive in the stories we overheard at the dinner table, in the tension we felt when the bills came in the mail, in the way our parents responded to financial success or failure, in the comparisons they made, in the things they celebrated or criticized. These beliefs are built in moments—not necessarily traumatic ones, but formative ones: a denied request, a splurge that brought guilt, a raised voice over a credit card bill, a quiet resignation when an opportunity was lost for lack of funds.

And because they are inherited—not chosen—they often remain unexamined. We don't question them, not because they are true, but because they feel normal. They feel like reality. If you were raised in a household where struggle was constant and wealth was rare, it may feel natural to assume that financial security is something "other people" enjoy. If your childhood was filled with material abundance but emotional tension about status and appearances, you may carry a belief that wealth requires performance or perfection. These beliefs, like seeds planted in early soil, grow roots deep into your behavior—shaping how you spend, how you save, how you give, how you judge yourself and others.

And yet, while these beliefs are powerful, they are not immutable. They can be seen. They can be named. They can be questioned. But first, they must be acknowledged.

Start by asking: What beliefs about money did I absorb from my family—spoken or unspoken? Did money represent safety, control, freedom, shame? Was it talked about openly or kept secret? Were we always chasing it or always fearing it? Was wealth admired, envied, dismissed, or distrusted? What did it mean to have money? What did it mean to not have it? And how are those early messages still echoing in my current financial life?

These questions may seem simple, but their answers are often complex. You may discover, for instance, that you avoid investing not because you don't understand it, but because deep down, you associate investing with risk, and risk with recklessness—a belief passed down from a parent who once lost everything in a market crash. Or you may realize that you overspend not because you're irresponsible, but because you inherited the belief that generosity means saying yes to everyone, even at your own expense. You may notice that you sabotage your financial goals every time you start gaining momentum—not because you lack discipline, but because somewhere in your story, you learned that too much success makes you selfish, or different, or disconnected from those you love.

This is the quiet power of inherited belief: it doesn't need to shout. It only needs to whisper, consistently, in your moments of decision. And unless you bring it into the light, it will keep steering the wheel without your permission.

But here's the good news: once you see a belief, you are no longer ruled by it. You have a choice. You can hold it up, examine it, ask where it came from, what it cost you, and whether it still serves you. And if it doesn't, you can let it go—not with bitterness, but with clarity. Because beliefs are not facts. They are stories. And stories can be revised.

This process, of course, takes time. Unlearning is not a single decision, but a practice. It requires compassion, because some of your beliefs may be tied to people you love—parents, grandparents, mentors

—who shaped your understanding of the world. Letting go of those beliefs can feel like a betrayal. But it isn't. It's an honoring. It is saying, "I see where this came from. I see how it helped you survive. But I live in a different world now, and I get to write a different story."

And in doing so, you don't just free yourself—you interrupt the cycle. You prevent those beliefs from passing to the next generation. You create a new inheritance, one made not of fear or shame, but of awareness and intention.

Because ultimately, what we pass down to our children—and to ourselves—is not just money, but meaning. Not just assets, but attitudes. Not just the contents of a bank account, but the context in which they learn to earn, spend, save, and give. And if we can become conscious of the beliefs we've inherited, we can begin to shape what we leave behind—not just in dollars, but in wisdom.

The inheritance of belief is real. It is powerful. But it is also transformable.

And the moment you begin to ask, "What did I inherit?" is the same moment you begin to ask, "What do I want to pass on?"

Childhood Scripts and Financial Patterns

There is a quiet theater that plays behind the curtain of every adult life—a private stage where the lines we repeat, the habits we perform, and the decisions we make have often been rehearsed long before we were conscious of having a role at all. This theater is not built in adulthood, though adulthood gives it form; it is shaped in childhood, where scripts are written not by us, but for us, and where financial behaviors, though seemingly spontaneous in the present, are often echoes of lessons, warnings, or unspoken understandings that were passed on through years of watching, listening, and absorbing.

We like to imagine that as adults, we are free agents, that every financial decision we make—every swipe of the card, every investment, every budgeting choice—is the product of deliberate reasoning and conscious will. But the truth is, much of what we do with money is not new. It is repetition. It is reenactment. It is the performance of a script written when we were children—scripts we didn't choose, but which we now embody, sometimes word for word, sometimes in subtle gestures we don't even recognize as repetition.

These childhood scripts are not always verbal. Often, they are emotional. They are written in the pauses between words, in the tightness of a parent's face when discussing bills, in the hurried "we'll talk about it later" when a child asks if the family is okay financially. They are written in birthday presents that came with strings attached, in shopping sprees that followed arguments, in the silence that followed a job loss. And like all scripts, they create patterns—predictable, automatic sequences of thought and behavior that emerge when we encounter similar emotional cues in adulthood.

Consider the person who was constantly told "we can't afford that" during childhood—not as a simple truth, but as a phrase loaded with anxiety, shame, or resentment. That person may grow up to fear money, to associate spending with danger, even when their income is stable. Or they may develop the opposite pattern, overcompensating for that early scarcity by spending impulsively, determined never to feel that restriction again. Another child, raised in an environment where money was used as a reward for good behavior or achievements, may come to associate wealth with worthiness—believing, often unconsciously, that they only deserve to feel financially secure when they're performing well.

Some scripts are rigid, shaped by repetition so constant they feel like law. "You must always save." "Never trust anyone with your money." "Rich people are selfish." "Debt is evil." "Buying things for yourself is wasteful." These phrases, whether spoken outright or implied through action, settle into our nervous system like truth, even when they no longer serve us. And when adulthood offers us choices—when we can, in theory, rewrite the narrative—we often don't realize we're still operating under a childhood director's notes, following lines we didn't consciously agree to.

And it's not just what was said—it's what was modeled. A child who watches a parent obsess over coupons may internalize frugality not as a helpful tool but as a sign of scarcity and fear. A child who sees one parent hiding purchases from the other may absorb the belief that financial transparency leads to conflict, and thus grow into an adult who keeps money matters private, not out of secrecy, but out of emotional survival. A child raised in a household where financial instability was the norm may learn to spend money quickly, afraid it will disappear—because, in their world, it often did.

These scripts don't just influence behavior—they shape identity. They become part of how we see ourselves. "I'm just not good with money." "I always overspend." "I'm a saver, not an investor." These aren't just descriptions—they're roles we've been rehearsing for years. And the more we repeat them, the more real they feel, even when they don't align with who we truly want to become.

What makes these patterns so hard to break is that they are often emotionally anchored. That is, they are tied not just to logic, but to feeling—feelings of safety, shame, pride, rebellion, or belonging. And because money is rarely neutral, these emotional undercurrents run deep. Trying to change your financial behavior without addressing the emotional script behind it is like changing the wallpaper in a house with a cracked foundation—it may look different on the surface, but the structure underneath remains unchanged.

So how do we begin to unearth these scripts? How do we identify the patterns that are no longer serving us?

It begins with reflection, not judgment. Start by noticing your financial tendencies—especially the ones that show up during stress, conflict, or transition. Do you avoid looking at your accounts? Do you panic when money comes in and rush to spend it? Do you feel guilt after making a purchase, even when it's reasonable? Do you say yes to lending money even when you want to say no? These behaviors are clues— breadcrumbs that lead back to the stories written in your early life.

Ask yourself: When did I first feel this way about money? What did my caregivers teach me, intentionally or not, about spending, saving, giving, or earning? What emotions do I associate with money—security, fear, control, chaos, freedom? What was modeled for me in times of financial hardship? What did joy or celebration around money look like? What did failure look like?

This kind of inquiry takes courage, because it often brings up grief—the grief of realizing that some of what we've carried all these years was never really ours to begin with. The grief of acknowledging that the people who raised us, though loving, were shaped by their own pain, their own limitations. And perhaps most of all, the grief of recognizing how much time, energy, and opportunity we may have lost by living out someone else's story.

But with that grief comes power. Because once a pattern is seen, it can be changed. Once a script is identified, it can be edited. You are not bound to repeat the choices of those who came before you. You are not destined to live out a story that no longer fits. And the process of rewriting that story is not about blame—it is about reclaiming authorship.

Rewriting your script doesn't mean erasing your past. It means using it as source material— acknowledging the influence, honoring what helped you survive, and choosing what to keep, what to release, and what to reinvent. It means giving yourself permission to speak new lines. To create new responses. To write new scenes, even if your voice trembles at first.

And as you do, you'll begin to notice something powerful: the more conscious you become of your childhood scripts, the less control they have over your present. The financial decisions that once felt compulsive begin to feel optional. The behaviors that once defined you begin to dissolve. You start making choices not out of fear or repetition, but out of alignment with your values, your goals, your *now*.

That's how transformation happens—not all at once, but moment by moment, decision by decision, breath by breath. Not through dramatic declarations, but through quiet awareness. Through the daily practice of noticing: *This is the old script. This is the new one I choose instead.*

Because you were handed a story—but you are not required to keep performing it. And once you realize that, a different kind of wealth becomes possible: the wealth of agency, of healing, of freedom.

Scarcity vs. Security – The Emotional Roots of Risk

Every financial decision, no matter how logical it may appear on the surface, is grounded in something far deeper than strategy—it is grounded in emotion. And perhaps no two emotions influence our financial lives more profoundly, more subtly, and more persistently than scarcity and security. They are not just feelings; they are frameworks. They are lenses through which we view opportunity, define risk, and interpret safety. They shape whether we approach money with clenched fists or open palms, whether we hoard or invest, whether we say yes to growth or retreat into fear. And the story they tell us—often inherited, often unconscious—becomes the emotional backdrop of every financial decision we make.

To understand why people react so differently to the same financial opportunity or threat, we must understand this emotional polarity: for some, risk feels like possibility; for others, it feels like threat. The difference is not in intellect or information—it is in emotional wiring, and that wiring is often rooted in early exposure to either scarcity or security.

If you grew up in an environment where money was tight, where bills were always looming, where financial emergencies were common and financial breathing room rare, then your nervous system likely learned to associate money with danger. Even in adulthood—even when your financial circumstances may have changed—that association doesn't always disappear. You may look at your bank account and see a healthy balance, but your body still remembers what it felt like to fear eviction, to hear your parents argue about expenses, to feel embarrassed when you couldn't participate in activities your peers took for granted. That emotional residue stays with you, and it whispers in the background of your decision-making: *Don't let your guard down. It could all disappear tomorrow.*

This is the emotional root of scarcity—not merely a lack of money, but a persistent, internalized sense that there will never be enough. Scarcity doesn't just say "you don't have enough now"—it says "you won't have enough later." It tells you to protect, to shrink, to delay, to doubt. It makes you suspicious of good fortune, skeptical of opportunity, and reluctant to take even calculated risks. It convinces you that safety comes not from growth, but from control. And while that mindset may have served you once—may have protected you from real, immediate harm—it can become a prison when your circumstances have shifted but your beliefs have not.

Conversely, those raised in environments of financial security—where needs were met consistently, where money was treated as a neutral or even empowering subject—may develop a completely different emotional relationship to risk. They may feel confident in their ability to recover from losses, to try new ventures, to ride out uncertainty. Their baseline isn't fear—it's stability. And from that place, risk feels tolerable, sometimes even exciting. When you are not constantly scanning for survival, you can afford to be curious, to be patient, to explore.

This is the emotional foundation of security—not arrogance or recklessness, but a quiet sense that you are supported, that you will be okay, that even if things don't go as planned, you will find a way through.

Security doesn't mean you take foolish risks—it means you don't collapse at the thought of temporary loss. It gives you perspective. It gives you space. And from that space, decision-making becomes expansive rather than reactive.

It is important to note that scarcity and security are not purely circumstantial. You can have very little money and still feel emotionally secure. You can have great wealth and still live in scarcity. Because these mindsets are not always about what's in your bank account—they are about what's in your belief system. And unless you examine that belief system, you may find yourself stuck in patterns that no amount of income or financial advice can fix.

For example, someone who lives in a scarcity mindset might save obsessively but never invest, convinced that the market is too volatile and that loss is inevitable. Another might refuse to leave a soul-draining job because they cannot imagine a world in which financial risk leads to anything other than disaster. Still others may undercharge for their work, overgive to others, or chronically put their own needs last, all because the emotional undercurrent says: *If I ask for more, it might be taken away. If I expect too much, I'll be disappointed. If I relax, I'll lose everything.*

These patterns are not just emotional—they are physiological. Scarcity activates the body's stress response. It floods the system with cortisol, narrows your focus to short-term survival, and limits your ability to engage in long-term planning or creative problem-solving. It is not a failure of willpower—it is a biological reaction, one that can't be reasoned with until it is first calmed, acknowledged, and understood.

The first step to shifting out of scarcity is not to tell yourself you're wrong. It is to recognize where it came from—and to offer yourself compassion for why it makes sense. Of course you're cautious about money if you grew up watching it disappear. Of course you flinch at the idea of risk if risk once meant hunger or instability. Of course you have a hard time trusting financial peace if you've never truly known it. These responses are not weaknesses. They are evidence of your adaptability. You learned how to survive in a context that demanded vigilance. That's not shameful—that's skillful.

But survival and thriving are different goals. And the habits that kept you afloat may now be the ones keeping you from swimming forward.

The goal, then, is not to eradicate caution, but to balance it with vision. To ask yourself, not just *what am I afraid of losing?*—but *what might I gain if I believed in the possibility of safety?* To begin slowly, gently stretching the edge of your comfort zone—maybe by investing a small, non-threatening amount, or by saying yes to an opportunity that feels both exciting and unfamiliar. To track not only your money, but your emotional responses to it: When do you feel fear? When do you feel shame? When do you feel peace? And what happens when you pause instead of react?

Equally, if you come from a background of emotional or financial security, your task may be different— but just as important. You may need to become aware of your privilege—not to feel guilt, but to develop gratitude and discernment. You may need to learn the difference between boldness and recklessness, between confidence and carelessness. You may need to listen more deeply to those whose decisions are shaped by very different fears—and offer empathy instead of judgment.

Because ultimately, security and scarcity are not fixed destinations. They are states that can shift, evolve, and influence each other. You can learn to cultivate emotional security, even if it wasn't your starting point. You can learn to recognize when fear is helpful, and when it is holding you back. You can begin to rewire your understanding of risk—not as something to avoid at all costs, but as something to understand, to measure, to engage with intentionally.

The emotional roots of risk are not found in spreadsheets—they are found in stories. In memories. In feelings that once kept you safe, and which now may be limiting your growth. And as with any root, the work of tending to it is slow, deliberate, and deeply personal.

But it is also freeing. Because when you begin to separate past fear from present reality—when you learn to say, *That was then, this is now*—you create the space to make decisions not from the place of who you were, but from the place of who you are becoming.

And that shift—from fear to awareness, from contraction to courage—is where real wealth begins.

How Family Narratives Shape Your Financial Future

Long before you open your first bank account or make your first real purchase, long before you understand the mechanics of interest or the concept of budgeting, you are already being shaped—not only by your environment or your circumstances, but by something even more subtle and potent: the ongoing narrative your family tells itself about money, success, struggle, and identity. This narrative may not be printed in a ledger or spoken in formal lessons, but it lives in the fabric of your home—in the stories repeated at the dinner table, in the comments made in passing, in the values subtly praised and quietly condemned. It is an emotional undercurrent, invisible but undeniable, and it forms the backdrop against which your financial mindset begins to develop, even in the earliest years of your life.

Every family has a story it tells about itself. Sometimes it is explicit, declared with pride or resignation: *"We're hard workers; we don't expect handouts."* Or *"We've always struggled, but we always make it through."* Or *"We come from nothing—we know the value of every dollar."* Other times, the story is more implied than articulated, passed on through expressions, behaviors, silences. It might sound like *"We're not the kind of people who invest,"* or *"That kind of lifestyle isn't for people like us,"* or *"We always take care of our own, no matter what it costs."*

These narratives shape your understanding not just of money itself, but of your place in the economic world. They tell you what's possible. What's admirable. What's expected. What's risky. What's selfish. What's honorable. What's achievable. And like all stories told often enough, they become scripts—scripts that define the roles you're supposed to play in your financial life.

If your family story is one of perseverance through hardship, you may feel a deep sense of pride in your ability to survive difficult times. But you may also struggle to feel comfortable with ease, success, or abundance. If your family glorified self-sacrifice and giving to others, you might grow into someone who feels guilty about keeping money for yourself, even when it's necessary. If your family saw wealth as corrupting or superficial, you may unconsciously sabotage your financial progress to stay in alignment with that belief.

These narratives don't just inform what you do with your money—they inform *who you believe you are* in relation to money. They define whether you see yourself as someone who thrives or someone who gets by. Whether you're destined for growth or survival. Whether you're allowed to dream beyond what your family could imagine, or whether you're tethered to their view of what's "realistic." And often, these narratives are enforced not by punishment, but by something more powerful: loyalty.

There is an emotional loyalty we often feel to the stories of our families—especially when those stories are rooted in struggle. If your parents worked multiple jobs to provide for you, you may feel conflicted about earning money with ease. If your family saw wealth as something reserved for others—outsiders, the lucky, the unethical—you may fear becoming estranged from them by aspiring to more. If your siblings continue to struggle financially, you may downplay your own progress or feel obligated to redistribute your resources so that you don't "leave them behind." And while these acts may stem from love, they can also create internal conflict—conflict between your desire to honor your roots and your longing to build something new.

This inner tug-of-war often goes unspoken. On the surface, you may say you want to grow, to invest, to achieve a new level of financial peace. But deep down, part of you may worry: *What does that say about me? Am I betraying where I come from? Am I abandoning the people who shaped me?* These questions don't always arrive as clear thoughts. More often, they appear as resistance. As hesitation. As self-sabotage cloaked in rationality.

This is the emotional weight of family narrative—it doesn't just shape what we believe, it shapes what we permit ourselves to pursue.

To move forward financially, you don't have to reject your family. But you do have to examine the story. You have to ask: *What is the narrative I grew up hearing about money? What roles did I see modeled—and which ones was I expected to play? What did my family celebrate? What did they fear? What was said about people who had money? What was said about people who didn't? What did success mean in our household— and what did it cost?*

You may discover that your family's story was one of resilience—but also of resignation. That it was filled with love—but also with limitation. That it taught you the value of hard work—but not the possibility of ease. That it praised generosity—but ignored boundaries. And all of that matters. Not to cast blame, but to create awareness. Because once you can name the story, you can begin to see when it's guiding your hand. When you're making decisions not from your current reality, but from an inherited narrative that may no longer serve you.

For example, if your family believed that money should never be talked about, you might avoid financial conversations in your own relationships, leading to miscommunication or secrecy. If your family equated frugality with morality, you may resist investing in yourself—even when it's wise. If your family warned against "getting too comfortable," you may constantly create new forms of struggle, unconsciously recreating the environment you knew best.

But here's the truth: you are allowed to evolve beyond the story you were given. You are allowed to write new chapters. You are allowed to say, *"That belief helped my family survive—but I want to thrive."* You are allowed to honor the strength of those who came before you while still choosing a different path. And doing so doesn't erase your roots—it strengthens them. Because when you grow, you expand what's possible not just for yourself, but for everyone watching, including those still trapped in old stories.

This kind of growth requires intentionality. It requires looking at the narratives you've internalized and asking: *Do I still believe this? Does this belief support the life I'm trying to build? Is this fear mine, or inherited? Is this value one I want to keep, or one I've outgrown?* These are not questions you answer once— they are questions you live with. They are questions that become the compass by which you navigate your own, self-authored financial life.

And over time, as you rewrite the narrative, something subtle but profound begins to happen: the past loosens its grip. The loyalty shifts from obligation to inspiration. The fear gives way to clarity. You stop trying to shrink yourself to fit a story written for someone else—and you start stepping into the story that's truly yours.

Because your family's narrative may have been the starting point—but it does not have to be the ending.

Rewriting Your Internal Money Dialogue

Some of the most powerful conversations we have in life are the ones that never leave our mouths. They are the quiet whispers that shape our decisions, the unspoken narratives that color our perceptions, the internal dialogues that play on repeat in our minds—especially when no one else is around to hear them. And when it comes to money, those inner voices can be the difference between peace and pressure, progress and paralysis, scarcity and sufficiency. Because whether we realize it or not, each of us has a running script—a personal, private conversation we carry inside us about what money means, what it says about us, and what we believe we deserve.

This internal dialogue didn't begin yesterday. It didn't arrive fully formed in adulthood. Like most things rooted deeply in our sense of identity, it was shaped over years, sometimes decades—by what we were told, what we observed, what we interpreted, and most significantly, by what we felt. And often, those feelings were not rational or even clear. They were emotional impressions, carried forward like baggage we forgot we were holding.

Some of us carry voices of fear—quiet, persistent thoughts like *"What if it all disappears?"*, *"I can't afford to relax"*, *"One mistake and I'll lose everything."* Others carry voices of guilt: *"I shouldn't have spent that"*, *"I don't deserve this level of comfort"*, *"Someone else needs this more than I do."* Still others wrestle with resentment: *"Why does it come easier for them?"*, *"I work just as hard, but I'm always behind."* And then there are the voices of inadequacy—the ones that whisper, *"I'm not good with money"*, *"I'll never figure this out"*, *"I'm not the kind of person who gets ahead."*

These internal narratives, repeated often enough, become emotional facts—things we stop questioning not because they're true, but because they feel familiar. And familiarity breeds attachment. Even when the message is harmful, even when it limits us, we cling to it because it gives us a sense of identity, of structure, of continuity. It becomes the lens through which we interpret our experiences, the filter that determines how we respond to success, failure, opportunity, or loss.

The irony, of course, is that most of these inner dialogues were never truly ours to begin with. They were passed down, picked up, absorbed from our families, our cultures, our peers, our environments. We did not choose them; we inherited them. But at some point, what we inherit becomes what we enact. And if we are not conscious of the scripts we're following, we will live out lives that reflect someone else's fears, someone else's limits, someone else's beliefs.

That's why rewriting your internal money dialogue is not just a financial exercise—it's an act of personal liberation.

But before you can rewrite, you have to *listen*. You have to tune into the quiet background of your financial decisions, the emotional soundtrack playing underneath your spending, saving, earning, and investing. You have to catch the script in real time—when you hesitate to invest in yourself, when you panic after making a necessary purchase, when you dismiss your financial accomplishments as luck, when you avoid checking your account out of shame or fear. Those moments are not just behavioral—they are conversational. Something is being said, internally. Something is being believed. And the first step toward change is to ask, *What is that voice actually telling me? And do I still believe it?*

This process requires honesty. It requires curiosity. And above all, it requires compassion. Because often, when we begin to examine our internal money dialogue, we discover just how hard we've been on ourselves. We discover that beneath the numbers lies a layer of criticism, of comparison, of deeply entrenched fear. We see that we've judged ourselves not just for what we've done, but for what we *felt*—for feeling insecure, unprepared, behind, envious, afraid. And in that judgment, we've created distance between who we are and who we want to be.

But judgment doesn't transform behavior—awareness does. Understanding does. Rewriting begins not with condemnation, but with acknowledgment: *Yes, this voice has been here a long time. Yes, it served a purpose. Yes, it helped me survive. But no, it no longer has to lead.*

The beautiful thing about dialogue is that it's not fixed. It's dynamic. It can evolve. And once you recognize that the conversation in your head is just that—a conversation—you can begin to respond differently. You can introduce a new voice. You can challenge the old one. You can speak back.

For example, if the voice says, *"You're irresponsible with money,"* you might respond with, *"I've made mistakes, but I'm learning. I'm creating systems now that support better choices."* If the voice says, *"You'll never catch up,"* you might counter with, *"I don't need to catch up—I'm allowed to move at my own pace."* If the voice says, *"You're not the kind of person who succeeds financially,"* you can say, *"That may have felt true once, but it's not who I am becoming."*

At first, these responses may feel awkward, forced, even dishonest. But so did the old voice—once. It became familiar through repetition. And so will the new one. The goal is not to pretend that fear or doubt no longer exist. The goal is to stop letting them have the final word.

This shift also means learning to speak to yourself with the tone you'd offer a close friend. You wouldn't tell a friend who's working hard to get out of debt that they're hopeless or lazy. You wouldn't shame someone you love for feeling anxious about a large purchase or for wanting to enjoy their money without guilt. You would reassure them. You would celebrate their efforts. You would remind them of their progress. So why not do the same for yourself?

Rewriting your internal money dialogue also involves giving yourself permission to imagine a new story— not just one of survival, but of sufficiency, of dignity, of expansion. That means letting go of narratives that only value struggle, that equate wealth with selfishness, or that demand you prove your worth through endless self-denial. It means allowing yourself to believe that peace is possible, that abundance doesn't require suffering, that your financial health does not have to come at the cost of your well-being or identity.

This kind of internal shift ripples outward. When you speak to yourself differently, you behave differently. You begin to make choices not from fear, but from alignment. You begin to set boundaries, not out of guilt, but out of self-respect. You start saving not as a punishment, but as an act of future self-love. You spend intentionally, give generously, receive graciously—not because a book told you to, but because the voice inside you has changed.

And as your internal dialogue evolves, so does your capacity to deal with external financial challenges. You become more resilient, not because you never doubt yourself, but because you've learned how to respond to that doubt. You no longer spiral when plans change or when numbers dip, because your worth is no longer tethered to your account balance. You've built something stronger than a budget—you've built a relationship with yourself that can weather uncertainty.

This is what true financial empowerment looks like—not perfection, not constant progress, but the ability to meet yourself kindly in the mess. The ability to catch yourself in old patterns and offer a new possibility. The ability to rewrite, not just what you do, but what you believe.

Because the most important money conversations you will ever have are not with your boss, your bank, or your accountant—they are with yourself.

And the good news is: you can change the script.

Chapter 3: Fear, Hope, and Everything In Between

If money were only about math, the world would look very different. Markets would behave predictably, budgets would be followed precisely, debts would be managed logically, and wealth would accumulate in line with intelligence and effort alone. But money is not about math—at least not primarily. It is about emotion. It is about stories, fears, hopes, and the complex terrain of the human heart. We want it to feel rational because that would make it controllable, but in truth, our relationship with money is often irrational, deeply emotional, and layered with feelings we struggle to articulate—especially when fear and hope are both present in the same breath.

Fear and hope—the two great emotional engines of our financial lives—do not live at opposite ends of a spectrum. They coexist. They pull and push at us, sometimes in tandem, sometimes in contradiction. Fear whispers caution, conjures worst-case scenarios, and roots us in survival. Hope reaches forward, imagines better tomorrows, and dares us to grow. One tells us to protect, the other tells us to pursue. And between them lies the full emotional spectrum of money—the tension of wanting more and fearing loss, of dreaming of abundance while guarding against ruin.

At first glance, it might seem that fear is the more dangerous of the two, the one that keeps us small, that convinces us not to invest, not to ask for a raise, not to believe we're worthy of financial peace. And it's true—fear can be paralyzing. It can keep us clinging to outdated stories and reactive behaviors. It can lead to inaction, to over-saving without joy, to under-earning out of self-doubt, to mistrusting opportunity even when it knocks gently and repeatedly.

But hope, too, carries its shadows. Unchecked hope can lead to recklessness, to trusting promises that are too good to be true, to spending on dreams instead of planning with discernment. Hope can be seductive

—it dresses itself in confidence and tells us everything will work out, even when we haven't done the work. It can cause us to dismiss risk too easily, to put faith in shaky ventures, to say "yes" when what we need is a strategic "no." In this way, hope—just like fear—can lead us into financial decisions that don't serve us, especially when we mistake wishful thinking for grounded optimism.

The real challenge is not to rid ourselves of fear or hope. It is to learn how to hold both. To sit in the tension between caution and courage, between the need to protect and the desire to expand. To recognize when fear is signaling something valuable—when it is asking us to pay attention, to slow down, to consider more carefully—and when it is simply echoing an old wound or outdated belief. To understand when hope is calling us to rise—to take a leap, to say yes to growth—and when it is masking avoidance, magical thinking, or desperation for rescue.

Because most financial decisions are made in this emotional gray zone—not in clarity, but in uncertainty. We want to feel certain before we act, but money rarely gives us that luxury. Markets fluctuate. Life happens. Emergencies don't RSVP. And so we find ourselves making decisions in the midst of uncertainty

—guided not just by numbers, but by the stories we tell ourselves about what might happen, what we fear losing, and what we hope to gain.

This is why two people can look at the same financial situation and come to completely different conclusions. One sees risk; the other sees potential. One sees a threat to be avoided; the other sees a door to walk through. And the difference lies not in intelligence or even in resources—it lies in emotional interpretation. In the way fear and hope are calibrated within each person's internal compass, often shaped by their past, their values, and their sense of self.

For some, fear is a constant companion—always nearby, always asking, *"What if it doesn't work?"*, *"What if I fail?"*, *"What if I never recover?"* For others, hope is louder—dreaming in full color, planning in leaps instead of steps, craving the feeling of breakthrough more than the reality of consistent progress. And most of us oscillate between the two—shifting our weight from one foot to the other, trying to find balance in a world that keeps moving beneath us.

Neither emotion is wrong. In fact, both are essential. Fear keeps us from jumping without a parachute. Hope reminds us that we can build wings on the way down. Fear asks us to protect what matters. Hope invites us to imagine something bigger. The goal is not to silence one in favor of the other, but to integrate them—to create a dialogue between caution and conviction, between groundedness and possibility.

And that integration doesn't happen in theory. It happens in real life—when the rent is due and the unexpected car repair wipes out your savings. When you're deciding whether to leave a job that pays well but slowly erodes your spirit. When you're weighing whether to invest in your own education, or to keep playing it safe. These are not spreadsheet decisions. These are heart decisions. And they require emotional literacy—the ability to notice what you're feeling, to name it honestly, and to respond with intention rather than reaction.

Emotional literacy also means giving yourself permission to *feel* without judgment. To admit that you're afraid without assuming that fear is weakness. To acknowledge your hope without assuming you're naïve. Because often, the most unhelpful thing we do in financial decision-making is not feel too much—but feel something and then shame ourselves for it. *"I shouldn't be scared—it's just money."* Or *"I shouldn't be so optimistic—I always screw things up."* These inner criticisms don't build wisdom; they build confusion.

And confusion leads to stagnation.

Instead, imagine asking yourself: *What am I actually afraid of? And what is this fear trying to protect me from?* Or *What am I hoping for? And what would it look like to move toward that hope with care, rather than blind faith?* These questions are not just reflective—they are revolutionary. Because they bring you back to the center of your own power—the space where you can choose how to act, rather than being swept away by unexamined emotion.

Over the next five subchapters, we'll explore this emotional landscape in more depth—starting with the biology of fear and how it hijacks our decision-making process, then moving into the double-edged sword of hope, the chronic overthinking that paralyzes even the most intelligent among us, the emotional flooding that occurs during high-stakes decisions, and finally, the tools and practices that allow you to master your emotions before they master your money.

But before we dive into those specifics, let this truth settle into your awareness: your emotional responses to money are not obstacles to overcome—they are signals to be understood. They are messengers. And if you learn how to listen without judgment, they will show you exactly where your healing begins, where your strength resides, and where your future is patiently waiting.

Fear and hope are not enemies. They are part of your emotional team. And when guided wisely, they can walk alongside you—not to hold you back, but to help you move forward with clarity, courage, and compassion.

The Fear of Losing vs. The Joy of Gaining

In the world of financial behavior, there is a curious imbalance that governs more of our decisions than we care to admit—an emotional asymmetry that tilts our judgment, clouds our logic, and often dictates the entire trajectory of our economic lives. It is the simple yet powerful fact that, for most people, **the pain of losing is felt far more intensely than the pleasure of gaining**. And this imbalance is not merely theoretical or anecdotal; it is embedded deep within the architecture of the human brain, wired into our most primal instincts of survival and security.

You may not remember every time you made a good financial decision—those steady months of saving, the smart investment that grew slowly, the time you chose needs over wants—but you almost certainly remember the times you lost something. The moment the market crashed. The guilt after an impulsive purchase. The sinking feeling of overdrawing your account or missing an opportunity you were too afraid to take. These memories are sticky. They hold emotional weight. And that weight influences every choice that comes after.

Behavioral economists call this phenomenon **loss aversion**, and while the term may sound clinical, its real-world consequences are deeply human. Simply put, we are more driven to avoid loss than we are to achieve equivalent gain. The possibility of losing $100 is more emotionally disturbing than the pleasure we feel in gaining $100. The same amount of money, but vastly different emotional reactions. And that skewed emotional ratio has ripple effects that stretch far beyond our wallets.

It explains why we hold on to failing investments longer than we should—because selling means admitting defeat. It explains why we're hesitant to switch jobs, even if the new offer is better—because the familiar feels safer, even when it's no longer serving us. It explains why we avoid starting new ventures, trying new strategies, or embracing bold ideas—because the *potential* for loss, even if small, eclipses the *potential* for gain, even if significant. We'd rather stay in the shallows of "what's known" than swim into the deep water of "what's possible."

But this isn't because we're irrational. It's because we're human. Our evolutionary blueprint was designed to prioritize survival, not satisfaction. In the ancestral world, failing to notice a threat could mean death. Missing an opportunity for abundance? That was less critical. As a result, our brains developed a negativity bias—a tendency to react more strongly to danger than to reward, to fear than to joy, to loss than to gain. This bias may have kept our ancestors alive, but in a modern economy, it can quietly sabotage our potential.

The fear of losing is not inherently bad. Like all emotions, it has a role to play. It keeps us cautious when we should be, reminds us to do our due diligence, protects us from recklessness. But when fear becomes the dominant lens through which we view all financial decisions, it distorts reality. It whispers, *"Better to stay where you are than risk going further."* It tells us that security is preferable to growth, that stability—no matter how stagnant—is more noble than curiosity, that comfort is better than expansion.

On the other side of this imbalance lies the joy of gaining—an experience that, while powerful, is often surprisingly short-lived. We dream of what it will feel like to achieve a financial goal, to pay off the debt, to land the raise, to hit the savings milestone. But when it finally happens, the euphoria is often brief. We feel relief, maybe even pride—but then, quickly, a new goal takes its place. A new fear arises. The gain fades into the background, while the fear of losing what we just earned moves center stage.

This cycle—of anticipating joy, briefly tasting it, then replacing it with new anxiety—is exhausting. And yet we repeat it, not because we enjoy it, but because we don't know how to interrupt it. We've been taught to measure progress in milestones and numbers, not in internal peace. We celebrate gains, but we don't know how to *stay* with them, how to savor them, how to let them shift our identity and rewrite the fearful scripts we've carried for so long.

What would it look like to give the joy of gaining as much emotional space as the fear of losing? To allow moments of progress to imprint as deeply as moments of loss? To let success expand us, rather than shrink back into caution the moment we taste it?

This doesn't mean becoming careless. It means becoming conscious. Conscious of when fear is valid—and when it's a leftover echo from past pain. Conscious of when caution is strategic—and when it's simply self-sabotage in disguise. Conscious of the fact that most of the time, the losses we fear are not fatal—they are emotional bruises, not existential threats.

And it also means learning to cultivate the *feeling* of gain, not just the fact of it. Because while losses trigger immediate, visceral reactions—sleepless nights, stress, panic—gains often require *intentional* celebration. They don't demand our attention; they ask for it gently. If we are not present with our wins, they fade unnoticed, and the emotional balance remains lopsided. We become people who remember pain more vividly than progress, who brace for the worst even in the midst of the best.

To change this requires more than affirmations. It requires emotional rewiring. It means pausing after every small financial victory—not just the big ones—and acknowledging it fully. It means tracking not only your expenses, but your emotional growth—how often you made decisions from wisdom instead of fear, how many times you resisted panic and chose presence, how frequently you honored your long-term vision instead of reacting to short-term noise.

It also means redefining what "loss" really is. Because not all losses are bad. Sometimes losing money teaches you discipline. Sometimes a failed investment opens the door to better strategies. Sometimes spending on yourself—even if it doesn't yield a financial return—creates emotional freedom that no number could match. When you stop seeing loss as failure and start seeing it as feedback, fear loses some of its grip.

Likewise, not all gains are inherently good. Not if they come at the cost of your values, your peace, your relationships, or your health. Not if they only fuel the next round of pressure, the next rung of the ladder you never actually wanted to climb. The joy of gaining is real, but it is most nourishing when it's aligned with who you are—not just what you've been told you should pursue.

Ultimately, the path toward financial maturity is not one of fearlessness. It's one of balance. It's the capacity to feel fear without being ruled by it. To pursue gain without becoming addicted to it. To see both loss and success as teachers, not tyrants. To walk the middle ground between caution and courage, knowing that the most important asset you'll ever manage is not your bank account—it's your emotional awareness.

Because the truth is, you will lose sometimes. That's part of growth. And you will gain, too. That's part of life. But the deeper truth is this: what you *feel* about those moments will shape you far more than what actually happened.

So give your victories a voice. Let them speak louder than your fear. And the next time you stand at the edge of a decision, ask not only *"What do I have to lose?"* but *"What do I have to gain—and what would it mean to finally let that joy be louder?"*

Why Hope Can Be as Dangerous as Panic

We've been taught, for most of our lives, to fear panic and to chase hope. Panic, with its sweaty palms and racing heartbeat, is the villain of our financial stories—the emotion that makes us sell at the bottom of the market, avoid taking chances, or run from risk even when it's calculated. Hope, on the other hand, wears the hero's cape. It tells us to believe in possibility, to move forward when logic says no, to keep our chin up even when everything feels uncertain. But what we don't often admit—perhaps because it sounds too cynical or too complicated—is that **hope, like panic, can be dangerous when left unchecked**, and that sometimes, it is not fear that sabotages us, but blind optimism dressed in inspiration.

To understand this, we must first distinguish between grounded hope and delusional hope. Grounded hope is an ally—it is built on reality, supported by data, and paired with action. It says, "I believe this can work, and I'm willing to show up for it." It acknowledges the effort required. It respects risk. It sees obstacles, but chooses to walk forward anyway—with both eyes open. Delusional hope, however, is a seductive liar.

It whispers, "Everything will be fine," even when nothing is changing. It encourages us to trust luck instead of systems. It turns red flags into rose-colored dreams. And it convinces us that belief alone will bring us the life we want, without the discomfort of discipline, the grind of growth, or the inconvenience of reality.

Hope becomes dangerous when it becomes an excuse. When it tells you not to look at your bank account because "something good is coming." When it tells you to invest in that too-good-to-be-true scheme because "you deserve a break." When it convinces you to ignore the mounting credit card balance because "it will all work out in the end." These are not financial strategies—they are coping mechanisms. And while hope feels better than panic in the moment, its consequences can be just as devastating, just as disorienting, just as irreversible.

Panic leads to paralysis. But false hope leads to passivity. And passivity is its own form of danger, especially in a world that rewards clarity, action, and awareness. When we're passive, we wait for change instead of initiating it. We expect rescue instead of building resilience. We scroll instead of planning, dream instead of doing, and wish instead of working. Not because we're lazy, but because hope has sold us a version of the future that doesn't require us to fully show up in the present.

There is also a cultural element at play here—one that celebrates positive thinking so loudly that it often silences anything that feels like doubt, caution, or realism. We are bombarded with messages that say, "Think rich," "Visualize abundance," "Manifest your dream life." And while mindset is undeniably important, the danger comes when mindset replaces method. When the belief in success takes the place of actual steps toward it. When someone drowning financially is told to simply "stop thinking poor," instead of being given tools, education, or structural support. In this light, hope can become toxic—a shiny distraction that keeps us from dealing with the truth.

And the truth matters. Financial health, like physical health, requires diagnosis before treatment. If you ignore the symptoms because you hope they'll go away, you may feel better temporarily—but eventually, the consequences catch up. Likewise, ignoring financial reality—overspending, avoiding debt, under-saving

—because "something will shift" is not courage. It is denial wrapped in optimism. And while panic may feel like fire, false hope is like smoke—it suffocates slowly, silently, without triggering alarm until it's too late.

This is not to say we should stop hoping. On the contrary—hope is essential. It gives us vision. It helps us endure seasons of lack. It fuels our goals, connects us to something bigger than the moment we're in. But we must learn to examine our hope. To ask where it's rooted. To ask what it's paired with. Because **hope without a plan is fantasy**. And fantasy is fragile—it shatters at the first sign of reality.

So what does examined, healthy hope look like?

It looks like building an emergency fund, not just visualizing wealth. It looks like tracking your spending, even when it's tight—especially when it's tight—because clarity is more powerful than avoidance. It looks like asking for help when you're overwhelmed, instead of pretending everything is fine. It looks like believing in your ability to grow financially, while also acknowledging that the path may be longer, harder, or messier than expected.

Healthy hope says, "I believe in better, and I'm willing to participate in creating it." It does not wait passively. It shows up. It adjusts when needed. It listens when fear speaks and responds with strategy, not denial. It knows that progress is not always linear, that setbacks are not signals to quit, and that true abundance is not just about money—it's about honesty, alignment, and emotional integrity.

It also recognizes when hope is being used as an emotional escape. Because sometimes, the most hopeful thing you can do is not to dream bigger—but to wake up. To stop repeating the same unhelpful patterns. To stop ignoring the habits that keep you stuck. To stop pretending that "tomorrow" will fix what you keep postponing today.

And in that awakening, something powerful happens: you stop hoping instead of acting, and you start hoping alongside acting. You let hope fuel your courage, not your complacency. You allow it to inspire structure, not replace it. And slowly, you begin to build a financial life that is not based on reaction—not to panic, not to fantasy—but on alignment with your values, clarity about your numbers, and commitment to your growth.

It's worth noting, too, that hope can be dangerous not just on the individual level, but on a collective one. Many financial crises—from housing bubbles to market crashes—were fueled not by fear, but by overconfidence, by excessive optimism, by a belief that "this time is different" and that the rules no longer apply. Entire economies have suffered because too many people trusted the illusion of endless gain and ignored the risks beneath. And while most of us are not making policy decisions or running billion-dollar funds, we still absorb the cultural mood. We're influenced by what everyone else seems to believe, even when our gut tells us to pause.

This is why emotional literacy is so important. Not just the ability to feel hope or fear, but to question it. To ask: "Where is this emotion taking me?" "What decisions is it leading me toward?" "Is it aligned with truth, or is it a way to avoid discomfort?" These questions don't kill hope—they refine it. They make it stronger, smarter, more useful. They turn it from a soft cushion into a sturdy foundation.

And ultimately, that's what we want. Not to get rid of hope, but to ground it. To strip it of illusion and fill it with discipline. To stop using it as a drug and start using it as a tool. Because when hope is mature, it becomes something more than emotion—it becomes strategy. And strategy builds futures that fantasy never could.

So yes, be hopeful. But be honest, too. Be realistic. Be ready to act. Let your hope be informed, not inflated. Let it challenge you to grow, not lull you into stillness. Let it coexist with fear, with doubt, with every messy part of the process. Because hope is not the opposite of panic—it is what we build when we move through panic, when we face truth, and when we choose to keep going—not because we're sure we'll win, but because we've decided we're worth the fight.

Anxiety and Overthinking in Financial Decisions

There is a peculiar kind of paralysis that often creeps in when the stakes feel high and the outcome uncertain—a mental loop so deceptively logical yet emotionally exhausting that it masquerades as diligence, when in fact, it is often fear in disguise. We call it analysis. We call it preparation. But what it frequently becomes, especially in matters of money, is **overthinking**, and beneath its surface lies a force even more insidious: **anxiety**.

Anxiety in the financial realm is not always a dramatic breakdown or a visible crisis. More often, it's a quiet undercurrent, a constant hum beneath the surface of our daily decisions—a feeling that no matter how much we plan, save, research, or prepare, something could still go wrong, something could still be missed, something could still unravel. It is the mental noise that turns a simple budget into an existential riddle, a small purchase into a guilt-laden debate, and a future goal into a maze of what-ifs too overwhelming to navigate.

What makes financial anxiety particularly tricky is its ability to camouflage itself as "being responsible." We tell ourselves we're just trying to make a smart choice, to be thorough, to protect ourselves from mistakes—and while those intentions are admirable, they often tip into a cycle of overthinking that leads not to clarity, but to decision fatigue, inaction, or self-doubt. The mind spins in circles, analyzing every possible scenario, every potential outcome, every worst-case deviation from the plan—and in doing so, it exhausts the very clarity we were seeking to find.

In many ways, overthinking is the anxious person's attempt at control. If I can just gather *enough* information, consider *enough* perspectives, wait for the *perfect* moment, then I can be sure I won't mess this up. But perfection is a mirage, especially in the world of money. No financial decision comes with complete certainty. Markets shift, needs change, unexpected events occur. And when we wait for the illusion of perfect safety before making a move, we often miss the windows that were more than good enough.

The problem is not thoughtfulness—it's thought loops. Thinking about your money is not a flaw; it's a strength. But when that thinking becomes obsessive, circular, or paralyzing, it no longer serves you. It becomes a trap disguised as logic. You replay the same arguments in your head. You compare yourself to others. You scroll for new opinions, seeking external validation. You hesitate, not because you lack intelligence, but because you've learned to distrust your own ability to decide—and that learned distrust often begins long before the current decision you're facing.

Perhaps you grew up in a household where money was a source of tension or unpredictability—where one wrong move led to a month of stress, where mistakes were punished or ridiculed, where financial confidence was absent or discouraged. In such environments, anxiety becomes a survival skill. You learn to anticipate problems, to imagine threats, to never relax around money. Even when you're safe. Even when you're doing fine. Even when nothing is technically wrong, your nervous system is still bracing for something to go wrong.

And so when you face a financial decision—whether to invest, to spend, to save, to change jobs, to start a business—that survival script reactivates. You begin to overthink not because the decision is actually dangerous, but because it *feels* dangerous. The stakes feel exaggerated. The options feel loaded. The possible consequences feel catastrophic, even if they're not. And that feeling, when left unexamined, becomes the lens through which you view every financial choice.

What's most cruel about anxiety is how it convinces you that *more thinking* will lead to peace, when in fact, it often leads to more spinning. You run scenario after scenario through your mind like a movie director trying to control every plot twist, but the story never resolves. Instead of making the decision and moving forward, you stay stuck in limbo—afraid to act, afraid to stop thinking, afraid of regretting whatever path you choose.

This is not a failure of intelligence. On the contrary, many people who struggle with financial overthinking are highly intelligent, conscientious, and well-informed. But the problem is not knowledge—it is the emotional *meaning* attached to the knowledge. When money becomes a reflection of your worth, your safety, your success, your competence, or your identity, every decision becomes emotionally loaded. You're not just deciding what to do with your money—you're deciding what kind of person you are, and whether that person will be okay.

And so the stakes feel sky-high, even for small choices. You debate whether to buy the laptop now or wait for a better deal, not because the price difference will change your life, but because you fear choosing "wrong." You avoid opening your investment account because you're not sure you made the best choices. You hesitate to book a trip or take a class or invest in yourself, not because the expense is irrational, but because the act of deciding without certainty feels intolerable.

To interrupt this cycle, you must first recognize that certainty is not the goal—**self-trust** is. The truth is, most financial decisions don't have one perfect answer. They have a range of good-enough choices, each with their own trade-offs. And when you understand this, your anxiety can begin to loosen its grip, because the pressure to find the one "right" path disappears. You're allowed to choose something that's *wise enough* for who you are, where you are, and what matters most to you—not something that's universally optimal.

Second, you must begin to separate thinking from spiraling. One is strategic; the other is self-soothing. Thinking involves gathering information, evaluating options, weighing pros and cons. Spiraling involves replaying fears, second-guessing your intuition, and delaying action in the hope that emotional clarity will magically appear. But clarity is not a precondition for action—it is often the *result* of it. You gain clarity by *doing*, by *trying*, by *deciding*—not by circling the runway endlessly, hoping for the perfect landing.

Third, create rituals that ground you. Overthinking thrives in ambiguity. It multiplies in silence. But when you introduce structure—whether through budgeting, journaling, talking with a trusted advisor, or setting clear decision deadlines—you reduce the mental static. You create containers for your thoughts, instead of letting them swirl aimlessly. Even simple practices, like limiting your research time or writing down your top three options with pros and cons, can help restore a sense of control. Not over the outcome—but over your process.

And perhaps most important, give yourself permission to make imperfect decisions. Not reckless ones— but human ones. You are allowed to choose based on values, not just numbers. You are allowed to learn as you go. You are allowed to change course later. And you are allowed to define "success" not as getting everything right, but as staying engaged with your financial life instead of abandoning it to fear.

Anxiety and overthinking are not flaws to eliminate—they are signals to understand. They arise when you care deeply about your life but haven't yet built the emotional infrastructure to trust yourself within it.

And that trust is built not by always making the perfect choice, but by surviving the imperfect ones. By seeing that you can make a decision, face its outcome, and still be okay. Still be growing. Still be you.

Because the greatest cost of financial anxiety is not lost money—it is lost peace. Lost time. Lost opportunities. The chances you didn't take. The relief you postponed. The version of yourself you haven't met yet, because you're still caught in mental rehearsals for a performance that never begins.

So next time you find yourself overthinking a financial decision, pause. Breathe. Ask: *Am I seeking truth, or avoiding fear? Am I gathering wisdom, or delaying discomfort?* And then, when you're ready—not when you feel certain, but when you feel grounded—choose. Move. Act. Trust.

The math may matter. But the moment you trust your own capacity to handle what comes after—that is when anxiety begins to fade, and ownership takes its place.

Emotional Flooding and Bad Timing

There are moments—sudden, unpredictable, and often inconvenient—when emotion overwhelms thought, when clarity is swallowed whole by a storm of sensation, and when decisions that should be weighed with calm consideration are made in the heat of impulse. This state is known as **emotional flooding**, and when it collides with financial choices, the results are almost always regrettable. Because timing, in money as in life, is not just a matter of the clock or the calendar—it is also about the **emotional weather** within us.

Emotional flooding occurs when the nervous system is overwhelmed—when the brain's higher reasoning functions are temporarily hijacked by intense emotion. You may experience it as a wave of panic, frustration, anger, desperation, or even excitement so intense that it drowns out the quieter voice of reason. You know you're flooded when your breath shortens, your mind races, your focus narrows, and your need for resolution becomes urgent, even desperate. It is in this altered state that we are most vulnerable to making bad financial decisions—decisions driven not by strategy, but by the raw instinct to escape discomfort.

The irony is that many of these decisions don't *look* impulsive in the moment. They feel justified. They feel *necessary*. You hit "buy" on a last-minute vacation you can't afford, telling yourself you "deserve it." You pull your money out of an investment after one dip, convinced that it's about to collapse. You apply for a loan in the middle of a panic, believing that more money will soothe the unrest inside you. But the truth is, these decisions are not about the numbers—they are about **regulation**. They are attempts to regulate the emotions you haven't yet learned to sit with.

Bad timing, in financial behavior, often doesn't stem from ignorance. It stems from emotion. A rational mind knows that selling low is unwise, that spending in a rage won't solve anything, that waiting for clarity is better than acting from chaos—but in the moment of flooding, rationality is drowned. And because modern life gives us so many tools to act instantly—one-click purchases, instant transfers, digital portfolios—we no longer have the built-in friction that might once have protected us from our worst emotional impulses.

The problem isn't emotion. Emotion is not the enemy. In fact, emotion contains wisdom—signals about what we value, what we fear, what we need to address. But when emotion becomes a tidal wave, and we respond to it without pause, we often make decisions that are not aligned with our long-term values, but are instead shaped by our immediate need for *relief*. Relief from uncertainty. Relief from fear. Relief from that internal voice that says, *"Fix this now, or something terrible will happen."*

To understand emotional flooding is to understand that the moment in which you feel most pressured to act is often the worst possible moment to do so. Because timing is not only about opportunity—it's about **readiness**. And readiness is not just about having the facts—it's about having the internal stability to weigh those facts clearly. You may be factually ready to invest, to buy, to launch, to restructure—but if you are emotionally hijacked, your mind is not prepared to make the kind of decision that respects your bigger picture.

Imagine a storm sweeping across the ocean—waves rising, wind howling, visibility reduced to chaos. That is the internal state of emotional flooding. Now imagine trying to steer a ship in those conditions—setting a course, adjusting the sails, making strategic choices. It's absurd. The only wise choice in that moment is to anchor, to ride it out, to wait until the sea settles enough to see clearly again. The same principle applies to emotional decision-making. When flooded, the first task is not to decide—it is to regulate. To pause. To ground. To wait.

This is not easy, especially in a culture that celebrates decisiveness and action. Waiting can feel weak. Slowing down can feel like falling behind. But wisdom is not measured by speed—it is measured by **alignment**. Acting from alignment requires you to *know* when your inner state is clear and when it is clouded. It requires humility. Patience. And the emotional intelligence to recognize that your urgency may not be truth—it may simply be fear wearing a costume.

One of the most dangerous features of emotional flooding is its ability to distort time. In a flooded state, *now* feels like *forever*. The discomfort of this moment feels permanent. You can't imagine it changing. So you act, hoping to end it. But what if you could remember that emotions are temporary—even the intense ones? What if you could recognize that your panic, your anger, your excitement, your sorrow—while real

—are not trustworthy guides for irreversible financial decisions?

This is especially important because many financial choices *are* irreversible—or at least very difficult and costly to undo. You can't unwithdraw your savings if you needed them later. You can't reverse a mortgage decision made in an emotional frenzy. You can't erase a spending spree once the bill comes due. And while regret can teach us, it is a brutal and expensive teacher—one that we can often avoid simply by learning to **wait out the storm**.

Developing this skill—emotional timing awareness—requires practice. It begins with noticing the signs of flooding. Are your shoulders tense? Is your breath shallow? Are your thoughts spinning? Do you feel rushed, trapped, cornered? Are you replaying worst-case scenarios or fantasizing about instant rescue?

These are signs that your system is overwhelmed. Not bad, not shameful—just a signal that this is not the right time to choose. It is the right time to **pause**.

In that pause, you can regulate. Breathe deeply. Step away. Journal. Walk. Talk to someone who knows how to hold space without judgment. Give yourself the gift of emotional distance from the urgency. Not to delay action indefinitely—but to protect your future self from choices made in the shadows of reactivity.

And here's the beautiful truth: most good financial decisions will still be there tomorrow. The opportunity, the idea, the investment, the change—it rarely requires immediate action. And if it does, it probably wasn't aligned with your real stability to begin with. Urgency is rarely a friend to wisdom. When you slow down, you don't lose power—you reclaim it. You return to a place where your *mind* and *body* are working together, not in opposition.

Over time, you begin to recognize your patterns. Maybe you flood after arguments. Maybe after long days. Maybe when faced with uncertainty. Maybe when you're tired, or lonely, or craving control. Knowing your triggers gives you freedom—not to avoid emotion, but to navigate it with grace. You build a kind of emotional compass that says, *"This feeling is strong, but it's not final. I will return to clarity. And I will decide from that place—not from this storm."*

This doesn't mean you'll never make mistakes. It doesn't mean you'll never feel flooded again. But it means you'll begin to trust yourself more deeply—not because you never feel overwhelmed, but because you've learned how to respond to it with wisdom instead of urgency. You'll learn to distinguish between real intuition and emotional noise. Between grounded clarity and survival instinct. Between good timing and reactive timing.

Because ultimately, financial peace is not built only on knowledge, but on **emotional regulation**. On the ability to hold space between stimulus and response. On the practice of pausing when it feels hardest. And on the quiet courage to trust that waiting, when done wisely, is not inaction—it is preparation.

So the next time you feel overwhelmed, desperate, impulsive, or euphoric—remember: this is not your moment to choose. This is your moment to anchor. To listen. To breathe. And to trust that the clarity you crave is already on its way—just beyond the storm.

Mastering Emotions Before Mastering Markets

We live in a time where information is abundant, where the mechanics of investing, budgeting, and financial planning are accessible to anyone with a smartphone and a working internet connection. There are thousands of tutorials, hundreds of financial "gurus," apps that automate wealth-building strategies, and algorithms that claim to beat the market. And yet, in this age of instant financial wisdom, most people are not failing because they lack access to data—they're failing because they haven't yet mastered the one thing that algorithms can't compute: **emotion**.

It is tempting to believe that success in financial markets is mostly a function of intelligence. That if we just read the right books, follow the right experts, subscribe to the right newsletters, or model our behavior after the most disciplined investors, we'll unlock the secret formula. But history tells another story—one in which even the brightest minds, the most disciplined planners, and the best-laid financial strategies can crumble in the face of **emotionally driven behavior**.

Because before there is the market, there is *you*. Before there are price charts, trends, forecasts, and compound interest tables, there is your body, your nervous system, your fears, your insecurities, your ego, your desires. And no matter how well you understand the numbers, if you haven't learned to regulate what happens within you, those numbers become meaningless at the moment they matter most.

Mastering emotions is not about repressing them or pretending they don't exist. It's about developing a respectful relationship with them—a relationship in which you can hear their message without being ruled by it, in which you can sit with fear without fleeing from it, in which you can feel the urge to act impulsively and still choose to wait. Because **emotional mastery doesn't mean eliminating feeling—it means restoring choice in the presence of feeling.**

Consider the behavior of people during a market crash. Logic says, "Stay the course." Every textbook says not to sell at the bottom. Every financial planner echoes the same principle: "Markets recover." But emotion says, "Get out now." Fear makes the screen look redder. The pain of loss feels immediate and personal. The desire to regain control overtakes every spreadsheet in the world. And so people sell—not because they don't know better, but because knowing better and doing better are governed by entirely different parts of the human experience.

Likewise, in times of rapid market growth, greed whispers that this time is different. Caution is dismissed. People invest in assets they don't understand, using money they can't afford to lose, simply because they fear being left behind. They tell themselves they're being strategic, but what they're really doing is trying to escape a deeper discomfort—the discomfort of watching others succeed while they wait. Again, the decision is emotional, not intellectual.

This is why emotional literacy must come before financial literacy. Because until you understand your emotional wiring—how you respond to uncertainty, how you react to loss, what triggers your impulsive behavior, what stories you tell yourself about money—you will always be vulnerable to the hidden forces inside you. You'll make decisions in the name of logic, but they'll be driven by emotion. You'll justify choices that were made in a rush of adrenaline or a fog of anxiety. You'll call it "gut instinct" when it's really fear. You'll call it "strategy" when it's really hope.

And so the real journey of financial mastery begins not with understanding the market, but with understanding the self. It begins with introspection, with asking hard questions:

- What does money represent to me—freedom, safety, validation, control?

- What are my earliest memories about money, and how do they shape my current beliefs?

- When do I feel most reactive around financial decisions—and what emotion is underneath that reaction?

- Do I avoid financial planning because it feels overwhelming, boring, shameful, or revealing? • Am I chasing wealth, or running from fear of scarcity?

These are not the kinds of questions you'll find on a balance sheet. They don't have exact formulas. But the answers you uncover will shape *how* you interact with every other financial concept you encounter. Because if money is a mirror, your behaviors are reflections—not of your intelligence, but of your inner world.

To master emotion is to stop outsourcing your self-worth to the performance of your portfolio. It's to stop treating every loss as a personal failure, every gain as a validation of your identity. It's to stop tying your sense of security to numbers that fluctuate daily and begin rooting it in something more durable—self- awareness, groundedness, and clarity of values.

In practical terms, emotional mastery might look like stepping away from your investment app when you're feeling anxious, instead of checking it obsessively. It might look like pausing for 24 hours before making a big purchase, especially when you feel triggered. It might look like not making financial decisions late at night, when your willpower is depleted and your thinking is reactive. It might look like setting up automatic savings because you don't fully trust your future moods.

But emotional mastery is not only about controlling reactivity. It's also about cultivating emotional environments that support long-term thinking. Calm, patience, curiosity—these are emotional states that create space for wise decisions. You nurture them not by accident, but by design. You build a life where you're not constantly on edge. You sleep enough. You move your body. You surround yourself with grounded people. You consume less noise and more clarity. These habits aren't just wellness practices— they are the hidden infrastructure of good financial behavior.

And it's important to recognize that emotional mastery is not a one-time achievement—it's a daily practice. Like any practice, some days are better than others. There will be moments when emotion wins. When you panic. When you spend too much. When you lash out at a partner about money. When you overcommit or underprepare. That doesn't mean you've failed. It means you're human. And every emotional misstep is not a signal to shame yourself—it's a signal to learn, to reflect, and to refine.

Because ultimately, emotional mastery isn't about perfection—it's about recovery. How quickly can you return to center after being thrown off? How compassionately can you observe your reactions without identifying with them? How honestly can you name your emotion and still move forward with intention?

The paradox is this: the more you work with your emotions, the less they dominate you. The more you build a language around your emotional experience, the less scary it becomes. And the less scary it becomes, the more freedom you have to make decisions based on what matters—not what panics you.

Financial independence is often presented as a number. But emotional independence—the ability to respond instead of react, to delay gratification, to stay grounded in chaos—is what allows that number to *mean* something. Because what good is a million-dollar portfolio if it's held by someone constantly at war with their own mind? What good is financial freedom if you're still emotionally enslaved by the same fears, triggers, and insecurities that haunted you before?

So yes—read the books. Study the markets. Build the strategies. But never forget: before you master the charts, the budgets, and the interest rates, you must learn to master the storm inside. Because your emotions don't need to disappear—they need to be understood. And once you can sit with them, listen to them, and guide them instead of obeying them, that's when the real transformation begins.

That's when money stops being a battleground—and becomes a tool. Not for proving your worth, not for escaping fear, but for building a life that reflects who you truly are beneath the noise.

Chapter 4: The Ego Cost of Wealth

We often think of money in material terms—figures in a bank account, assets on a statement, items in a shopping cart. But beneath the surface of wealth lies a far more subtle and powerful force, one that rarely shows up in ledgers or spreadsheets yet dictates much of what we do with our money: **ego**. And while ego is not inherently evil—it is, after all, part of the human experience—it becomes dangerously expensive when left unchecked. Because unlike compound interest or inflation, the ego's cost is rarely visible. It doesn't show up as a line item. It shows up as a life out of alignment.

In many ways, money is the most socially visible scoreboard we have. We can't see someone's inner peace, emotional maturity, or kindness at a glance—but we can see the car they drive, the neighborhood they live in, the brand on their wrist. And in a culture where perception is often mistaken for value, where comparison is wired into our digital environments and self-worth is tethered to metrics, money becomes more than a tool—it becomes a symbol. A symbol of status, of importance, of success. And that's where ego enters the room.

The ego thrives on image. It craves significance. It wants to matter—and to be seen as someone who matters. And in the absence of a grounded internal identity, it will latch onto whatever external markers it can find to build a sense of self. Money, in this case, becomes a mirror—not just of our means, but of our **insecurities**, our ambitions, our hidden wounds. When we don't know who we are without it, we begin to use it to become someone else. Or worse, to prove to others that we already are.

The danger here is not ambition. It is not the desire to succeed, to grow, or to provide well for ourselves and those we love. The danger is the subtle shift from *using* money to *define* ourselves to *needing* money to *validate* ourselves. And that shift often happens without us even noticing. It shows up in the way we overspend to keep up appearances, in the way we feel inadequate next to someone else's highlight reel, in the way we delay joy until our income reaches a certain threshold, or in the way we treat financial setbacks as personal failures rather than circumstantial challenges.

And so we find ourselves chasing—not just financial stability, but **financial superiority**. We compete with people who don't even know we're in a race with them. We scroll through curated images of success and mistake them for reality. We say things like, "I'll feel better once I make six figures," or "I just need to prove I can do it," not realizing that the peace we seek has nothing to do with the numbers and everything to do with the **narratives** we've attached to those numbers.

This is the ego cost of wealth—the cost of living a life curated for applause rather than authenticity. It is the cost of pursuing what looks good at the expense of what feels good. Of accumulating things that signal success, while quietly feeling like we're never quite enough. And because the ego is insatiable, the finish line keeps moving. You buy the car, and now you want the upgrade. You move into the new house, and suddenly your furniture feels outdated. You reach the salary goal, and immediately start calculating how much more you *really* need.

The irony is that the more we chase wealth for egoic reasons, the poorer we often feel inside. Because ego doesn't measure *enoughness*—it measures *comparison*. And comparison is a game you can't win, because someone will always have more. Someone will always seem farther ahead. Someone will always post a better photo, buy a bigger house, get a better return on investment. And when your self-worth is tied to staying ahead, you become financially rich but emotionally bankrupt.

What's even more exhausting is that ego doesn't just demand more—it demands visibility. It wants recognition. So it nudges us to spend, not just to satisfy ourselves, but to ensure others *see* us satisfying ourselves. It whispers that quiet success is insufficient, that modesty is invisibility, that true wealth must be displayed to be validated. And in this way, it pushes us toward choices that may be financially unwise but socially rewarded. It turns investing into gambling, saving into deprivation, and generosity into performance.

But beyond the external pressures lies an even deeper tension—the **internal split** between who we are and who we're pretending to be. When we spend to impress, when we earn to prove, when we chase success as a way of silencing our doubts, we slowly disconnect from ourselves. We begin to live through a persona crafted for validation rather than truth. And that disconnection, while subtle at first, eventually becomes unbearable. Because no amount of wealth can fill the void left by the absence of self-honesty.

It's not that money and ego must always be enemies. In fact, self-awareness around ego can lead to more intentional wealth-building. But this requires the courage to ask difficult questions—questions that strip away image and reveal motive. *Am I making this purchase because I value it—or because I want to be seen as someone who does? Am I working harder because it fulfills me—or because I'm afraid of looking like I'm falling behind? Am I chasing this financial goal because it's aligned with my vision—or because I'm trying to prove I'm worthy?*

These questions are uncomfortable. They threaten the stories we've built about success. But they're also liberating. Because once you disentangle ego from wealth, you gain the freedom to define success on your own terms. You stop competing with people who aren't watching. You stop buying things you don't need to impress people who don't care. You stop trying to win a game that was never worth playing.

Instead, you begin to operate from a place of **internal clarity**. You choose investments that match your values, not your image. You spend in alignment with your life, not your Instagram feed. You stop needing applause because you've learned how to sit with silence. And you discover that the deepest form of wealth isn't about being admired—it's about being *free*.

This chapter is a mirror held up to the hidden costs of ego in our financial lives. It will explore how pride and insecurity distort our decisions, how comparison becomes a trap, how the need to impress leads to chronic dissatisfaction, and how humility—not arrogance—is often the secret weapon of lasting success. You'll come to see that ego is not something to eliminate, but something to **understand, manage, and occasionally silence**, so that your financial life reflects your real values—not just your desire to win approval.

Because at the end of the day, wealth that feeds the ego will always be hungry. But wealth that feeds the soul—that comes from a place of groundedness, purpose, and humility—has a way of nourishing you far beyond the numbers in your account.

Competing with People Who Aren't Watching

There's something strange—almost absurd—about the way we engage with money in the modern world, especially when filtered through the ever-present lens of comparison. Though we rarely admit it aloud, many of the choices we make about how we spend, save, invest, or earn are not truly rooted in personal desire or long-term vision—they are, instead, shaped by a silent, invisible game we play against people who are neither aware of our competition nor invested in the outcome. We buy the car to match our neighbor's. We renovate the kitchen because someone on Instagram did. We aim for a salary goal that sounds impressive at reunions, but never asked ourselves whether that number actually matches our real needs or dreams. And so we move through life measuring ourselves by standards no one set for us, racing toward victories no one else is watching.

This quiet competition becomes especially dangerous because it masquerades as ambition. On the surface, it looks like motivation—it pushes us to work harder, strive further, set goals. But underneath it, there is something much more hollow: the desire to *not lose* a race that doesn't exist. To not fall behind in a marathon we didn't consciously enter. To not be the one who looks like they're settling, struggling, or "less than" in the eyes of people we may not even like, trust, or respect.

What fuels this behavior is not always arrogance, but often insecurity—a subtle, persistent belief that our value is conditional, that our worth is somehow determined by how we stack up against others. And in a world where people curate their lives for public consumption, where success is filtered and staged, and where everyone's highlight reel is visible with a single swipe, it becomes all too easy to fall into the trap of **accidental competition.**

We rarely ask: *Who am I really trying to impress?* Because if we did, the answers might embarrass us. A former classmate we haven't spoken to in ten years? A sibling with different dreams and values? A stranger on the internet who follows us but doesn't know us? It sounds ridiculous when spoken aloud, but this is precisely how the ego works—quietly, subtly, and often without our full awareness. It tells us that to be worthy, we must win at something. And in the absence of a clearly defined finish line of our own, we default to someone else's.

The tragedy of this game is that there is no peace in winning. Because even when you reach the milestone you thought would silence the self-doubt—whether it's a salary, a home, a title, or a lifestyle—you quickly realize that someone else is still ahead. Someone is always ahead. And so the measuring continues. The upgrade becomes the new baseline. And you never quite feel the satisfaction you were chasing, because you weren't actually chasing fulfillment—you were chasing approval. And approval is a currency that devalues quickly.

There is a cost to this competition, and it is not merely financial. Yes, it might lead to overspending, overworking, or overcommitting—but beyond that, it creates a slow erosion of authenticity. You begin to shape your financial life around other people's expectations rather than your own values. You make decisions to avoid perceived failure rather than to pursue genuine purpose. You start to ask, *"What will they think?"* more often than you ask, *"What do I actually want?"* And over time, that disconnection becomes a kind of quiet despair—the sense that you're achieving without meaning, succeeding without joy.

And the people you're competing with? They're not watching. They're consumed by their own versions of the same game. The colleague whose career path you're trying to mirror is secretly doubting her own. The entrepreneur you admire is battling burnout. The influencer with the luxury lifestyle is deep in debt.

Everyone is looking sideways, and no one is looking inward. And so we all keep running—faster, harder, without asking where the finish line is or whether it's even ours to cross.

This doesn't mean competition is inherently bad. Healthy comparison can spark inspiration. Seeing others achieve can open our imagination to what's possible. But the line between *inspired by* and *defined by* is dangerously thin. When comparison fuels creativity, it's a gift. When it fuels self-doubt, it becomes poison. The difference lies in whether we're grounded in our own vision, or floating in someone else's.

The antidote to this invisible race is not withdrawal—it is **intentional clarity**. It is the quiet but courageous act of stepping back and asking, *What is enough for me?* Not for my parents. Not for my peers. Not for the algorithm. For me. What does success look like, feel like, sound like in *my* life, given *my* values, *my* circumstances, *my* aspirations?

This question sounds simple, but it is one of the most radical things you can ask in a world that profits off your comparison. Because once you begin to define "enough" on your own terms, you start to reclaim your financial agency. You no longer need to buy to feel worthy. You no longer need to prove anything through possessions. You no longer chase numbers that don't align with your true needs. You begin to build a life—not an illusion.

Sometimes that life looks simpler than others might expect. You might earn less and be happier. You might choose time over income. You might drive a modest car while owning your schedule. You might live in a smaller house and travel the world. Or you might choose stability over scale. These choices make sense when you are no longer comparing them to someone else's highlight reel—but rather aligning them with your own **inner compass**.

Because the real cost of competing with people who aren't watching is not just money—it is the slow death of alignment. It is waking up in a house you bought to impress someone who isn't even in your life anymore. It is wearing clothes that feel like a costume. It is showing up to work every day to maintain an image you no longer care about. It is performing instead of living.

But there's another way. And it begins with permission. Permission to stop racing. To step off the scoreboard. To let others pass you if they want to. To pursue a life that makes sense to your heart even if it confuses the crowd. To live in a way that feels deeply satisfying rather than momentarily impressive.

You don't have to win a race no one is watching. You don't have to chase validation that changes with every scroll. You don't have to let your money choices be dictated by silent comparisons and imagined judges.

Instead, you can choose authenticity over approval. Vision over vanity. Peace over performance.

And once you do, your financial decisions become clearer. Your spending becomes more conscious. Your goals become more honest. And slowly, steadily, you begin to feel something that money can't buy—but which, paradoxically, gives money its meaning: freedom.

Impressing Others Is Expensive

There is a strange irony that lingers beneath the surface of our financial decisions, a quiet contradiction that governs many of the ways we use money, and yet remains largely unspoken: the fact that we often spend, not to improve our lives, but to manage the perceptions of others. We buy the upgraded car, not because our current one is broken, but because we imagine how we will look driving it. We choose the premium version of things not because we truly value the difference, but because we want to broadcast our status, our success, or our belonging. And while we may justify these choices with rational explanations, deep down, many of them are made in service to a silent audience. An audience that, most of the time, isn't even paying attention.

The cost of impressing others is not limited to the price tag on luxury goods or lavish vacations—it extends far deeper, infiltrating our financial well-being, our emotional balance, our personal values, and even our sense of self. When money becomes a means of image management rather than a tool for freedom or fulfillment, it becomes not only expensive in dollars, but also in energy, time, and authenticity.

The truth is, trying to impress others with what you have is like pouring water into a bucket with a hole in it—no matter how much you pour, it never feels full. Because the moment you base your satisfaction on someone else's admiration, you've given away your agency. You've made your sense of worth conditional, not on what matters to *you*, but on what others might *think* of you. And that's a losing game, because perception is both fickle and fleeting.

What makes this even more exhausting is that the standards we are trying to meet are often imaginary. No one ever handed us a rulebook that said, "You must own a home by 30," or "Your wedding must cost

$40,000 to be valid," or "Success means flying first class and wearing designer shoes." These are narratives we've absorbed passively—from media, marketing, peers, family, and culture—and we've internalized them so deeply that we've stopped questioning them. Instead of asking, *Does this align with who I am?*, we ask, *Will this make me look successful?* And so we spend—often beyond our means, often beyond our needs—not for utility or joy, but for applause.

But applause is noisy and short-lived. One moment you're admired, the next you're forgotten. Someone else shows up with more, with better, with newer. The crowd moves on, and you're left holding the bill. And if you're not careful, the habit of spending to impress becomes a cycle—one in which your self-worth is constantly held hostage by external validation, and your finances are drained by the need to project a version of yourself that might not even exist.

This is why impressing others is so expensive: it creates a **lifestyle of performance**. Every purchase becomes a costume. Every upgrade becomes a script. Every financial decision is filtered through the question, *"How will this look?"* rather than *"What do I need?"* or *"What do I value?"* And performance is exhausting. It requires constant maintenance. It demands that you stay on trend, stay ahead, stay relevant. And as the cost of that performance rises, your freedom shrinks. You begin to work not to live, but to maintain the illusion. You save less, not because you can't afford to, but because saving is invisible and spending is loud.

This doesn't mean you must live frugally or deny yourself pleasure. But it does mean you must become radically honest about your **motives**. Are you dining at that restaurant because the experience delights you

—or because you want to be seen there? Are you buying that handbag because you love its craftsmanship

—or because it signals status to others? Are you booking that trip because it aligns with your dreams—or because you imagine the photos will earn admiration?

The answers to these questions don't have to be perfect. We are social creatures, and part of us will always care, to some degree, about what others think. But the danger arises when that care becomes the compass by which we navigate our entire financial lives. When we abandon our own sense of value in pursuit of perceived value. When we mistake appearance for alignment.

And perhaps most heartbreaking of all is the quiet shame that follows this kind of spending. Because deep down, we know. We know when we've bought something just to prove something. We know when we've stretched ourselves for optics. We feel the dissonance between what we truly need and what we've pretended to need. But we often silence that voice, telling ourselves it's just part of the game, part of adulthood, part of modern life. And so the cycle continues—until one day, the weight of it all becomes unbearable. The debt piles up. The joy fades. The mask slips. And we're left wondering, *Was it worth it?*

There is another way. A quieter, freer, more grounded way. It begins with defining wealth, not as a performance, but as a personal experience. Not as what others see, but as what you feel. Maybe it's the feeling of walking into a home that fits your life—not one that merely fits a Pinterest aesthetic. Maybe it's the peace of knowing your bills are paid, your future is secure, and your choices are your own. Maybe it's the joy of spending on things that genuinely matter to you, even if they don't impress anyone else. That, too, is wealth.

The cost of impressing others disappears the moment you stop needing to. And that freedom is worth more than any luxury car or status symbol. Because when you are no longer performing, you begin to reclaim your energy. You begin to redirect your money toward things that build true value—like time, health, creativity, impact, and peace. You begin to spend with intention, not compulsion. You begin to see through the illusion that more always means better.

One of the most powerful questions you can ask before making any financial decision is this: *"If no one were to ever see this, would I still want it?"* If the answer is yes, then you are likely aligned with your values. If the answer is no, then you may be spending for someone else's gaze, not your own fulfillment.

Impressing others is expensive not because people are hard to please—but because the need to be pleasing is insatiable. There will always be someone with a bigger home, a flashier car, a shinier life. But none of that matters when your financial life is anchored in something deeper than image. When it's built on integrity, not imitation. On clarity, not comparison. On substance, not spectacle.

In the end, the most impressive people are not those who look rich, but those who live well—on their own terms, in alignment with their truth, free from the need to perform. Their homes may be simple. Their clothes may be unbranded. Their lives may be quiet. But their freedom, their peace, their joy—that's what wealth truly looks like.

Pride, Shame, and the Trap of Financial Identity

Somewhere along the winding journey of growing up—between childhood's innocence and adulthood's expectations—money stops being just a tool and becomes something far more complex: a mirror. A mirror that reflects not just what we have, but who we think we are, and, more importantly, who we believe we are *supposed* to be. And in that reflection, distorted by the expectations of culture, family, media, and memory, we often find ourselves tangled in two of the most potent and polarizing emotional forces: **pride** and **shame**. These twin emotions, though opposite in tone, operate along the same axis—they both define our identity in relation to our financial standing, and both create cages in which our true selves grow quietly distant.

Pride in money is not always loud. It doesn't always look like boasting or flaunting. Sometimes, it's quiet. Sometimes, it's the subtle sense of superiority we feel when our account is growing while someone else is struggling. Sometimes it's the validation we feel when a purchase proves we've "made it," or when our choices reflect the dreams our parents once whispered into our ears. Pride, in its healthiest form, is confidence rooted in discipline and alignment. But pride, when bloated by ego, becomes a blinder—it convinces us that we are our net worth, that success means being above others, that our value grows as our possessions multiply.

And the trouble with this kind of pride is that it turns financial success into identity. It whispers, "You are your salary." It seduces with praise. It grows in tandem with public recognition. And as it swells, it starts to make you fearful—not just of loss, but of visibility in loss. You don't just worry about losing money; you worry about losing the self-image that money has helped you build. You don't just fear setbacks; you fear what those setbacks will signal to others. And so your financial decisions become less about logic, strategy, or joy—and more about preservation of an image.

But what pride builds, shame is always waiting to dismantle. Because the moment you experience a reversal—a bad investment, a job loss, a mounting debt—pride, having been rooted in external validation, collapses, and shame takes its place. And shame is not just pain—it's identity erosion. It doesn't say, *"You made a bad decision."* It says, *"You are a failure."* It turns circumstantial hardship into personal flaw. And because money is such a visible aspect of our lives, shame around money often becomes debilitating, isolating, and corrosive.

You see it in the man who loses his job and can't bring himself to tell his family. You see it in the woman drowning in credit card debt, pretending everything's fine. You see it in the young adult who avoids reunions because they're not where they thought they'd be financially. These aren't just stories of struggle

—they're stories of *identity rupture*. Because somewhere along the line, we've come to believe that wealth equals worthiness, and financial missteps equal moral or personal failure.

But money is not a moral scoreboard. It is not a measure of intelligence, character, or goodness. It is a resource—one shaped by countless factors: upbringing, opportunity, culture, privilege, luck, timing, and sometimes, yes, discipline and effort. Yet we treat it as a mirror to the soul, and in doing so, we hand it far too much power.

And so we build our financial identity on foundations too fragile to hold the weight of real life. We become attached to roles: the breadwinner, the provider, the successful one, the investor, the entrepreneur. And when life inevitably shifts, when markets fall, when jobs disappear, when mistakes are made, we don't know how to decouple the event from our essence. We don't know how to say, *"I am still whole, even if I lost money."* Because the money wasn't just a tool—it was a self-definition.

What's most insidious is that both pride and shame push us into silence. Pride makes us hide our financial wins in layers of image and superiority, pretending it was all mastery rather than partly fortune. Shame forces us into secrecy, afraid to admit we're struggling, afraid to ask for help. And in both states, we become **disconnected**—from others, from truth, from ourselves. Pride isolates us atop a pedestal we're afraid to fall from. Shame isolates us in a hole we're too afraid to climb out of. And both block the vulnerability that leads to growth, the honesty that leads to healing, and the humility that leads to wisdom.

The trap of financial identity lies in its rigidity. When who you are is tied to a financial image, you stop evolving. You become defensive of your status. You avoid risks that might threaten your role. You filter your choices not through what you want, but through what your identity demands. The wealthy entrepreneur can't admit burnout. The high-earner can't take a break. The provider can't downsize. The successful investor can't change course. Because to do so would feel like betrayal—not of the finances, but of the self-image wrapped around them.

But what if we let go of that identity? What if we chose to define ourselves not by our income bracket, our possessions, or our outward image, but by something deeper—our character, our choices, our resilience, our capacity to learn and adapt? What if we saw pride not as a mask, but as a quiet knowing? What if we saw shame not as a life sentence, but as a signal—a signpost pointing to a wound that wants to be healed, not hidden?

Letting go of financial identity doesn't mean rejecting ambition or success. It means holding it loosely. It means being able to say, *"I built something, but I am not that thing. I lost something, but I am not that loss."* It means understanding that money flows, circumstances change, and your worth is not up for negotiation based on your bank balance.

One of the most liberating things you can do is to separate who you are from what you earn. To treat money as a tool—not a title. To experience both success and struggle without attaching them to your identity. Because when you do, you gain not just financial clarity, but emotional freedom. You're no longer afraid to admit when things are hard. You're no longer desperate to prove when things are good. You become anchored in something deeper than economic status—you become anchored in *truth*.

And from that place of truth, you begin to make better decisions. Not decisions fueled by ego, insecurity, or fear—but decisions aligned with values, goals, and purpose. You stop hiding behind pride, and you stop drowning in shame. You become honest—with yourself, with others, with your financial life. And in that honesty, you find peace. Because you're no longer performing. You're simply living. You're no longer defending an identity. You're simply being.

Money is important. But it is not you. It is not your identity. It is not your mirror. And it is certainly not your verdict.

Self-Worth vs. Net Worth

There is perhaps no confusion more damaging to our emotional and financial lives than the quiet, unspoken belief that our self-worth rises and falls with our net worth. It's a belief so deeply embedded in modern society, so cleverly reinforced by the way we speak about success, ambition, and value, that most of us don't even realize we've internalized it—until we find ourselves measuring our entire existence by numbers in an account, assets on a statement, or status in a social circle. And when we do, we create a life where our sense of being *enough* is constantly conditional, vulnerable to every shift in the economy, every perceived setback, every comparison that leaves us feeling small.

The truth is, money makes a poor mirror. It reflects what you have, not who you are. Yet, in the quiet corners of our mind, we begin to merge the two until we can no longer tell the difference. When the business is thriving, we feel competent. When savings are growing, we feel smart. When the home is large and the car is new, we feel important. But what happens when life changes course, as it often does? What happens when the deal falls through, the market crashes, the job disappears, the savings dwindle? If your identity was built on your financial achievements, then any loss feels like personal collapse. Suddenly, you're not just struggling financially—you're questioning your very worth as a person.

This is the danger of equating self-worth with net worth: it makes your value *conditional*. And conditional value is exhausting. You are always performing, always producing, always chasing some version of "enough" that keeps moving further away. Because as the numbers grow, so do the expectations. What once felt like success now feels like the new baseline. The house that once made you proud becomes "average." The income that once brought peace now feels insufficient. And so the race continues—not for joy, not for freedom, but for validation.

We learn this early. Children don't ask about emotional depth—they are praised for winning, for excelling, for being "ahead." As we grow, the language around money reinforces the illusion. We call high earners "worth more." We describe people as "successful" based on what they have, not who they are. We equate purchasing power with personal power. And in doing so, we teach generations that their humanity is measured in digits.

But what if it isn't? What if self-worth is something entirely separate—something intrinsic, unshakable, and untouched by external outcomes? What if it's not tied to productivity, performance, or profit, but to presence, integrity, and compassion? Imagine for a moment a world in which a person's value was based on their character, their kindness, their courage—not their cash flow. It sounds idyllic, even naïve, in a culture driven by consumerism. But that doesn't make it less true. It makes it less common. And what is rare is often the most valuable.

When we begin to see ourselves as more than our financial state, everything changes. We make decisions from a place of clarity, not desperation. We pursue goals because they align with our vision, not because we need them to prove something. We weather setbacks with resilience, because we know that loss is not identity. We stop apologizing for being in transition, for starting over, for having less, because we no longer see those things as shameful. They are simply *facts*, not verdicts. Experiences, not definitions.

It's important to understand that having high net worth is not the problem. The problem is when we *require* that net worth in order to feel like we matter. When we tie our peace, confidence, and dignity to financial metrics, we hand over our emotional sovereignty to forces we can't always control. The market is volatile. Jobs come and go. Success is often cyclical. And if we've built our self-esteem on these things, then we are guaranteed to live a life of emotional instability—feeling proud in abundance and ashamed in scarcity, always swinging between the extremes of ego and despair.

The goal is not detachment from money, but detachment from *identity in money*. It is the ability to say: *My value doesn't rise when my investments do, and it doesn't fall when I make a mistake. I am constant, even when my circumstances change.* That kind of inner stability is rare, but it is powerful. It makes you less reactive, more thoughtful. Less afraid of failure, more open to growth. And, ironically, it often leads to better financial outcomes—because you're not chasing quick fixes or proving points. You're grounded.

Consider this: when your self-worth is intact, you can say no to things that don't serve you, even if they're lucrative. You can leave jobs that drain your spirit. You can walk away from deals that compromise your values. You can live simply, without apology. You can build slowly, without shame. You can fail publicly, and still sleep well at night. Because you know that your identity is rooted in something deeper than success.

But this isn't easy. It requires unlearning decades of conditioning. It requires catching the voice in your head that says, *"You're falling behind,"* and asking, *"Behind what? Behind whom?"* It means being brutally honest about how much of your financial ambition is driven by desire versus how much is driven by insecurity. It means disentangling your goals from your need for approval. It means learning how to sit with discomfort, uncertainty, and even judgment—without crumbling.

And perhaps most importantly, it requires **compassion**. Compassion for yourself in all stages of life—when you're building, when you're thriving, when you're struggling, when you're starting again. Compassion that doesn't measure you against others, but honors your path. Compassion that reminds you: *You were always enough, even before the raise, the house, the title.* Because you were.

In a world obsessed with metrics, it is radical to anchor your identity in something unquantifiable. To say, *I matter, even when I'm not impressive. I'm valuable, even when I'm quiet. I'm enough, even when the world says I should be more.* That kind of belief is not weakness. It is strength. It is the foundation upon which sustainable success is built—not success that wavers with every external change, but success that stands regardless.

The real wealth is knowing who you are without the numbers. Because once you know that, money becomes what it was always meant to be: a tool. A powerful tool, yes—but just that. A means to an end, not the end itself. And the end is peace, freedom, purpose, presence, joy. These are the things that matter. These are the things money can support—but not replace.

Your net worth is a figure. Your self-worth is a truth. One can fluctuate. The other should not.

The Humility Advantage in Money Matters

In a world that often equates loudness with authority and certainty with strength, humility tends to be misunderstood—seen as weakness, passivity, or lack of ambition. Yet, when it comes to money, humility is not only a virtue; it is a **strategic advantage**—one of the most overlooked and underappreciated assets in the pursuit of financial well-being. Because while pride may blind, and ego may deceive, humility keeps your vision clear, your decisions grounded, and your path open to learning and growth.

Humility is not the denial of value. It is not about shrinking or apologizing for your success. Rather, humility is the quiet understanding that you do not know everything, that you are not invincible, and that even your best judgment is susceptible to error. In the financial world, where uncertainty is constant and variables are infinite, such a mindset is not only wise—it's essential.

A humble investor doesn't assume the market will always go up. A humble entrepreneur doesn't believe their instincts are infallible. A humble spender doesn't treat lifestyle upgrades as inevitabilities, but as conscious, measured choices. In every case, humility acts as a buffer against overconfidence—a trait that has toppled empires, drained fortunes, and led countless people into ruin. When you approach money with humility, you're not being timid—you're being smart.

Because the truth is, the financial world rewards long-term thinking far more than it rewards brilliance. And long-term thinking requires the emotional discipline to stay the course when things don't go your way. It requires the willingness to admit when you're wrong, to pivot when necessary, and to seek out better information even when it challenges your current worldview. None of these things are possible without humility. Pride clings to what it knows. Ego defends itself even in the face of failure. But humility adapts. Humility listens. Humility learns.

You see this difference most clearly in how people handle mistakes. Those who lack humility will deny their errors, double down on bad choices, or blame external forces. But those who are anchored in humility will reflect, recalibrate, and move forward wiser. And that kind of resilience builds financial endurance. Because money, like life, is unpredictable. And the people who do well over the long term are rarely the smartest or the boldest—they are the ones who remain teachable.

Humility also has the power to protect you from **comparison**, one of the most dangerous emotional traps in the realm of money. When you're secure enough to say, *"I don't need to match what others are doing,"* you free yourself from the pressure to overspend, overextend, or live a life that's not aligned with your values. You stop making decisions to impress. You stop chasing appearances. You begin to craft a life that fits *you*, not one that performs for someone else.

This internal confidence—born from humility, not bravado—gives you the rare ability to say no. No to the bigger house you don't need. No to the investment that feels too good to be true. No to the social pressures that demand you upgrade just to keep up. Humility doesn't say, *"I can't afford that."* It says, *"I don't need that to feel valuable."* And that mindset is incredibly powerful—because it shifts the narrative from acquisition to alignment, from proving to choosing.

Moreover, humility fosters **collaboration** and **curiosity**—two traits that are goldmines in the world of finance. When you're not threatened by not knowing everything, you're more willing to ask questions, to seek counsel, to learn from others without needing to dominate the conversation. You surround yourself with people who challenge your blind spots rather than echo your biases. And in doing so, you create an environment where better decisions are made—because they are rooted not in ego, but in exploration.

Perhaps one of the most surprising benefits of humility is its impact on **wealth preservation**. Many people are good at making money, but far fewer are good at keeping it. The reason is simple: when you begin to believe that your success is entirely due to your own genius, you start taking bigger risks. You assume the rules no longer apply to you. You stretch your bets. You ignore caution. And eventually, you fall. Humility, on the other hand, creates guardrails. It reminds you to diversify, to plan, to save, to prepare for downturns even when times are good. It is not pessimism—it is wisdom.

And let us not forget: humility also makes you more generous. When you understand that your success is not solely your own doing, but also the result of timing, opportunity, support, and sometimes even luck, you're more inclined to give back. You recognize that others might be struggling not because they're lazy or incapable, but because they haven't had the same chances. This perspective fosters empathy—and empathy is one of the most powerful forces in human connection. It makes you a better leader, a better friend, and yes, a better steward of your wealth.

Still, humility requires inner work. It requires letting go of the desire to be seen as impressive. It demands that you untangle your identity from your achievements. It asks you to sit with uncertainty without pretending you've mastered it. And in a society that rewards confidence—even when it's baseless—this can feel countercultural. But in the quiet corners of real life, where financial decisions have lasting consequences, humility is the difference between fragility and fortitude.

It also makes you more **adaptive**—because when your ego isn't driving the car, you're more willing to take unexpected turns. Maybe your career path changes. Maybe your investments evolve. Maybe your goals shift. Humility gives you the flexibility to pivot, to realign, to say, *"This no longer fits me, and that's okay."* Without the need to prove anything, you become free to follow what's true.

In the end, humility in money matters is not about thinking less of yourself—it's about thinking more clearly about yourself. It's about holding space for your brilliance without needing to brandish it. It's about making room for others, for change, for growth. It's about recognizing that even the most successful people in the world are still guessing, still learning, still vulnerable to error. And if they are, then surely, so are we.

The irony, of course, is that humble people often *do* become highly successful—not because they demand attention, but because they make consistently better choices. They are less likely to be reckless. They are more likely to stay in the game longer. They accumulate not just wealth, but wisdom. And over time, that wisdom compounds in ways no spreadsheet can measure.

So if you're looking for an edge in your financial life, start not with strategy, but with **self-awareness**. Not with confidence, but with **curiosity**. Not with ego, but with **humility**. Because in a noisy world where everyone is trying to be someone, the quiet power of staying grounded—of knowing that you don't have to prove, perform, or pretend—might just be the greatest advantage of all.

Chapter 5: The Myth of Rational Decisions

In theory, money should be the most rational domain of our lives. Numbers don't lie. Budgets are clear. Interest rates are measurable. Investment returns are trackable. In the world of spreadsheets, logic reigns supreme, and decisions—at least in principle—should follow a linear path of cause and effect, reward and risk, cost and benefit. Yet, the reality is far messier. Human beings, despite our pride in intelligence and innovation, are not logical machines. We are emotional creatures wrapped in stories, biases, instincts, and fears. We don't make financial decisions in a vacuum. We make them in living rooms filled with childhood memories, at dinner tables where guilt and pride linger, in boardrooms haunted by competition and approval, and in quiet late-night moments when fear whispers louder than reason.

This chapter exists to challenge one of the most dangerous myths in personal finance: the myth of rationality. The idea that we, armed with data and good intentions, consistently make the best possible choices. That we behave like economists predict—maximizing utility, minimizing loss, optimizing returns. In truth, we are far closer to behavioral creatures than rational ones. And the more we pretend otherwise, the more vulnerable we become—not just to poor financial outcomes, but to the shame that follows when we wonder why we couldn't stick to the budget, why we panic-sold in the dip, why we borrowed when we shouldn't have, or spent when we knew better.

Rational decision-making, as defined in economic theory, assumes perfect information, clear preferences, stable emotions, and a long-term view. But real life rarely grants us any of those luxuries. Most of us operate with partial knowledge, shifting priorities, and a mind cluttered by past wounds, social pressure, and subconscious fears. We tell ourselves stories about why we made a purchase or skipped a payment, but beneath those stories often lie deeper forces—unexamined beliefs, hidden insecurities, inherited behaviors, and psychological distortions that nudge our choices long before logic enters the conversation.

Consider, for instance, the person who knows they should be saving for retirement but can't seem to resist lifestyle inflation every time their income increases. Or the investor who panics at every downturn despite understanding the long-term strategy. Or the young couple who stretches their budget to buy a house in a better neighborhood—not for practical reasons, but because of subtle status anxiety and a fear of being seen as "less than." These aren't anomalies. These are the norms. And yet, we continue to label these decisions as irrational outliers rather than acknowledging the very human mechanisms behind them.

One of the core reasons this myth persists is because we overestimate the role of knowledge in behavior. We believe that if people *know* better, they will *do* better. But there's a vast canyon between intellect and instinct. Between knowing what's best and actually choosing it. And until we accept that gap—and understand the psychological terrain that fills it—we will continue to create financial systems, educational tools, and personal expectations that set us up to fail.

Financial education is important. But it's not enough. What's needed is *behavioral literacy*—an understanding of how our minds work under pressure, how our emotions shape our instincts, how our environments influence our decisions, and how we can create systems that support better outcomes not through willpower, but through design. In other words, we don't need more financial formulas. We need better self-awareness.

This chapter will explore that inner terrain. We'll begin by dismantling the illusion that we are primarily logical beings. We'll examine how emotion—not logic—is often the driver of choice, and how we rationalize decisions after the fact rather than reason them beforehand. We'll then move into the science of cognitive biases—those mental shortcuts that help us survive but often lead us astray. From the sunk cost fallacy to the anchoring effect, we'll explore the hidden forces that shape our choices and cost us dearly when left unchecked.

We'll also look at one of the most potent psychological drivers in finance: **loss aversion**—the tendency to fear loss more than we value gain. This single trait explains why people stay in toxic investments, avoid risks that could pay off, or sell too soon in a rising market. It's not that they don't know better—it's that the pain of potential loss is felt more vividly than the logic of potential reward.

Next, we'll confront the powerful echo chamber of **confirmation bias**, where we seek out information that supports our existing beliefs and ignore data that challenges them. In a world driven by social media algorithms and filter bubbles, this bias doesn't just affect our politics—it affects our money. It reinforces bad habits, prevents learning, and gives us false confidence in faulty decisions. To become better decision- makers, we have to learn how to seek dissent, challenge assumptions, and question our own narratives.

And finally, we'll explore the concept of building a **decision filter**—a personal framework that takes into account not only the numbers, but the emotions, values, and blind spots that influence your financial life. This isn't about perfection. It's about increasing the odds of success by designing systems that work with human nature, not against it. It's about recognizing that even when we *want* to be rational, we're often emotional first—and adjusting accordingly.

What makes this chapter essential is not just that it names the problem—but that it treats irrationality not as a moral failure, but as a universal reality. We all make decisions that don't make sense in hindsight. We all fall prey to impulses we later regret. But shame doesn't help us improve. Awareness does. Curiosity does. Humility does. The more we can understand our inner landscape, the more we can navigate it with grace, patience, and precision.

Ultimately, the goal isn't to become perfectly rational—it's to become **consciously irrational**. To know your patterns. To anticipate your weaknesses. To build guardrails that prevent your worst tendencies from derailing your long-term goals. Because the truth is, no one is immune to poor decisions—but those who are willing to examine their minds, to question their instincts, and to adapt their systems, give themselves a massive edge—not only in finance, but in life.

So let go of the myth. Let go of the illusion that you're supposed to make flawless decisions every time. And instead, embrace the reality that money is not a logic test—it's a reflection of your psychology, your environment, your memories, and your hopes. And when you learn to work with all of those forces— instead of against them—you begin to make decisions that are not only smarter, but also *truer*.

We Think We're Logical—We're Not

We like to believe we are the masters of our own decisions, guided by rational thought, clear logic, and objective reasoning. We imagine ourselves carefully weighing options, analyzing consequences, and selecting the most sensible path forward—especially when it comes to money, where the stakes often feel high and the outcomes measurable. We build spreadsheets. We read financial advice columns. We compare percentages and projections. And yet, time and time again, we make choices that defy our own knowledge. We spend when we planned to save. We invest in hype when we promised ourselves discipline. We take risks we can't justify and avoid ones we should probably embrace. The gap between what we *know* and what we *do* isn't just wide—it's fundamental. And at the heart of that gap lies the uncomfortable truth that, for all our intelligence, human beings are not primarily logical creatures.

We are emotional first, rational second—if at all. Our brains evolved to prioritize survival, not spreadsheets. Decisions that feel good often override those that make sense. And this tendency doesn't vanish with age, experience, or education. It doesn't matter how many books you've read, how much money you've earned, or how carefully you planned your future—your emotional mind still has the power to hijack your rational one, especially in moments of uncertainty, stress, or social comparison. The most dangerous thing is not that we are irrational. It's that we believe we're not.

This illusion of rationality is deeply ingrained, and perhaps nowhere more so than in the world of

personal finance. We've been taught to view financial decisions through a lens of logic. Save more than you spend. Diversify your investments. Avoid high-interest debt. These principles are simple enough to understand—and yet, millions of people who *understand* them still act against them. Why? Because logic is only one part of the decision-making equation, and often not the most powerful one.

Imagine this: you're at a car dealership, test-driving a vehicle that's slightly out of your budget. You did your research. You know what you can afford. You even told yourself, *"I won't go over this amount."* But the salesman is charismatic. The leather interior smells good. The upgraded sound system plays your favorite song. You start to imagine how you'll look driving it, how it will feel pulling into your driveway. Suddenly, logic gives way to emotion. You justify the higher price with talk of "safety features" and "long- term investment." But in truth, the decision was already made in your body—your brain is just scrambling to explain it.

This isn't a flaw. It's a feature of how we're wired. The emotional centers of our brain—particularly the amygdala—activate faster than the logical, analytical prefrontal cortex. Emotions come first.

Rationalization follows. And once an emotion is triggered—be it desire, fear, envy, or excitement—it can be incredibly difficult to override, even when the facts are clear. That's why you can read an entire book on compound interest and still raid your savings account for a vacation. That's why someone can understand the risk of speculative investing and still pour money into a meme stock because *everyone else is doing it*.

The truth is, we rarely make decisions in a vacuum. We are influenced by mood, fatigue, social context, and even the temperature in the room. Studies have shown that judges are more likely to grant parole after lunch. That people spend more money on sunny days. That investors make riskier decisions when their favorite sports teams win. These aren't anomalies. They are evidence that the human mind is far more context-dependent than we'd like to admit. And the more complex or uncertain the decision, the more likely we are to rely on emotional heuristics rather than deliberate analysis.

In finance, this manifests in countless ways. Consider the phenomenon of "anchoring"—the tendency to rely heavily on the first piece of information we receive. If someone tells you that a stock was once worth

$100 and is now trading at $50, you may feel it's a bargain—even if it's objectively overpriced. Why? Because your mind has latched onto the original number as a reference point, even though that number may have no relevance to the current reality.

Or think about "mental accounting," where people treat money differently depending on where it came from. A tax refund might be spent freely, while the same amount from a paycheck is carefully saved.

Rationally, money is money. But emotionally, it's not. The story we attach to it changes our behavior.

Then there's the "sunk cost fallacy"—a classic emotional trap. Say you've invested time and money into a business idea that clearly isn't working. Logic says cut your losses and move on. But your emotions say, *"I've come this far. I can't quit now."* The money you've already spent shouldn't affect your current decision

—but it does, because we hate the idea of waste, even if continuing means greater loss.

We're also heavily influenced by the people around us. Financial decisions are rarely made in isolation. We compare ourselves to peers, mimic trends, seek approval. We buy things we don't need to impress people we don't even like. We chase returns because someone at work bragged about crypto. We avoid risk because our parents were burned in a downturn. These aren't rational decisions—they're emotional reactions wrapped in social armor.

Perhaps the most subtle yet pervasive form of irrationality is our belief in our own immunity to it. We tend to think of *other* people as irrational—those who spend recklessly, invest foolishly, or live beyond their means. But we see *our* decisions as justified, informed, and reasonable. This is known as the bias blind spot—the tendency to recognize bias in others while denying it in ourselves. It's a dangerous illusion, because it prevents us from developing the humility necessary to question our instincts or to build systems that protect us from ourselves.

So what's the solution? How do we navigate a world that demands rational decision-making with a brain built for emotional survival? The answer is not to eliminate emotion—that's impossible, and even undesirable. Emotion is what gives meaning to our choices. It's what drives motivation, connection, and joy. The goal is not to become a robot. The goal is to become *aware*—to recognize when emotions are leading the way, to pause before reacting, to reflect before justifying, and to create safeguards that account for our very human tendencies.

This might look like automatic savings plans that remove willpower from the equation. Or investment strategies that are set and forget, so you're not constantly reacting to headlines. Or spending rules that limit impulsive purchases by building in a waiting period. These aren't signs of weakness—they are signs of wisdom. They acknowledge that we are not always the best judges of our own behavior in the moment, and they build guardrails accordingly.

Self-awareness is the foundation of rational financial behavior—not knowledge, not intelligence, not even experience. The most successful people in money aren't the ones who never make mistakes. They're the ones who know when they're most likely to make them—and plan around that. They understand that their mind is not a neutral calculator, but a deeply layered network of emotion, history, and instinct. And instead of pretending otherwise, they work with it.

It's also important to create space for reflection. To ask questions not just about the *what* of a decision, but the *why*. Why am I making this choice right now? What am I feeling? What am I afraid of? What story am I telling myself? Who am I trying to impress—or protect? These questions slow the process down.

They bring your conscious mind into the equation. And they help you discern whether you're acting from alignment or impulse.

In the end, recognizing that we are not as logical as we think is not an admission of failure—it's an invitation to wisdom. It's the first step toward making decisions that are not only smarter, but kinder to ourselves. Because when we accept that emotion is part of the process, we can stop blaming ourselves for every mistake, and start designing a life that works with our nature—not against it.

We are not robots. We are not calculators. We are complex, emotional, beautifully flawed beings trying to make sense of an unpredictable world. And when it comes to money, that truth is not a weakness. It is a compass. One that, when respected, can lead us to clarity, confidence, and ultimately, to peace.

Cognitive Biases That Cost You

Every financial mistake you've ever made—every purchase you regretted, every investment you chased too late, every opportunity you ignored until it was gone—was likely filtered through a lens you didn't even know was there. That lens is cognitive bias: the invisible framework of assumptions, shortcuts, and emotional distortions that shape how we see, interpret, and interact with the world. It's not always dramatic. In fact, it's usually subtle—quietly adjusting our decisions just enough to lead us away from logic and toward a conclusion that feels *true*, even when it isn't.

These biases are not flaws in a broken system. They are features of the human brain—a brain built not to process data objectively, but to react quickly in a complex and often unpredictable world. In the wild, thousands of years ago, these shortcuts were useful. They helped our ancestors make fast judgments: what to eat, where to run, who to trust. But in the modern world, especially in the world of money, these same shortcuts can sabotage our intentions without us even realizing it.

Let's begin with one of the most common: **confirmation bias**. This is our tendency to search for, interpret, and remember information in a way that confirms our existing beliefs. It's why a person convinced that real estate is the safest investment will ignore market downturns and obsess over success stories. It's why someone skeptical of stocks will downplay decades of consistent returns in favor of one story about a cousin who lost everything. We don't just look for truth—we look for validation. And in doing so, we become blind to alternatives that could save us time, money, and regret.

Confirmation bias is especially costly in investing. If you enter a trade already believing it will succeed, your brain will filter new data to protect that belief. Bad news? You'll say it's temporary. Mixed results? You'll call it noise. You become emotionally attached to being *right*, and that attachment clouds your ability to assess risk or pivot. The bias doesn't just distort your view of the market—it distorts your view of yourself. You stop asking, *What is the truth?* and start asking, *How can I prove I was right all along?*

Next comes the **anchoring effect**. Imagine walking into a store and seeing a coat priced at $500. That seems steep. But right next to it is another coat marked $900, now on sale for $500. Suddenly, the first coat feels like a bargain—even though it's the same price as before. That's anchoring: the first number you see sets a reference point that distorts your perception of value.

In finance, anchoring shows up everywhere—from real estate to stock prices to salary negotiations. Investors hold on to a stock simply because it was once priced higher. Homeowners overvalue their house because they remember what they paid, not what it's truly worth today. We cling to original prices, past highs, or arbitrary benchmarks as if they are facts, when in truth they are just psychological anchors— anchors that drag our decisions in the wrong direction.

Another major player in the world of financial distortion is the **sunk cost fallacy**—our tendency to continue investing time, money, or energy into something simply because we've already put so much into it. This fallacy traps people in bad investments, failing businesses, and relationships that no longer serve them. Logically, past effort should not influence present value. But emotionally, walking away feels like admitting defeat, like wasting all that has been sacrificed. So we keep going. We throw good money after bad. We hold the stock that keeps falling. We "wait just a little longer," hoping things turn around. But often, the smartest move isn't to persist—it's to let go.

Then there's **recency bias**, the mental shortcut that convinces us the most recent events are the most significant. If the market has been climbing for a few months, we assume it will keep climbing. If there was a sudden crash, we fear more crashes. This bias exaggerates the importance of what just happened and downplays long-term trends. It makes us overreact to short-term volatility, panic when things dip, and get greedy when they rise.

Recency bias clouds our ability to see patterns clearly. It's why investors get caught in bubbles and bail out during crashes. It's why people assume a bad year means a bad decade, or that a hot stock is a permanent winner. This bias narrows our time horizon to what's happening *right now*, which is dangerous—because wealth, real wealth, is built in *decades*, not *moments*.

Let's not forget **overconfidence bias**, perhaps the most seductive of all. Most of us believe we are better than average—better drivers, better investors, better decision-makers. This inflated self-view makes us underestimate risk, overestimate returns, and ignore contrary advice. Overconfidence leads to excessive trading, risky bets, and a false sense of control. It's the voice that says, *"This time, I know better,"* even when the evidence says otherwise.

In finance, overconfidence can be catastrophic. It convinces people they can time the market, pick winners, beat the pros. And sometimes they can—once. But over the long run, overconfidence tends to erode wealth faster than almost any other bias. It masks reality behind a wall of ego and blinds us to the very real limitations of our knowledge.

Also lurking in the shadows is the **status quo bias**—the tendency to prefer things as they are, even when change would benefit us. It's why people stay in bad financial habits, keep using poor budgeting tools, or avoid switching banks even when fees rise. Change, even positive change, requires cognitive effort. The path of least resistance is always to keep doing what we're already doing. So we stay where it's familiar. Safe. Easy. And in doing so, we often miss out on opportunities to grow, evolve, and optimize.

One of the most dangerous biases of all is **loss aversion**—which we'll dive deeper into in the next section. For now, it's important to understand that our fear of losing is stronger than our desire to gain. Losing

$100 hurts more than gaining $100 feels good. That imbalance leads people to avoid risks that are rational and to cling to security even when it's stagnating. It causes hesitation, indecision, and missed chances. It turns even minor volatility into emotional upheaval.

Now, none of these biases are inherently evil. They're simply tools our brain uses to simplify complexity. The problem is when we use them unconsciously—when we assume our instincts are accurate and our perceptions are objective. Biases aren't failures in character. They're just facts of psychology. But if we want to make better decisions, we have to bring them into the light.

So how do we do that?

First, we name them. Awareness is the first form of power. Once you can identify the bias influencing your behavior, you can pause. You can reflect. You can choose differently. For example, the next time you find yourself holding a losing investment out of loyalty, ask: *Am I staying because it's the best choice—or because I hate to feel like I've wasted something?* That single question can cut through the fog of the sunk cost fallacy and realign you with your actual goals.

Second, we create *systems* that bypass bias. Don't rely on willpower or good moods. Use automation. Use pre-commitment strategies. Use rules-based investing that takes emotion out of the equation. Instead of deciding when to save or invest based on how you *feel*, set up auto-deposits and stick to them regardless of market mood.

Third, we invite *external perspectives*. Talk to someone outside your emotional bubble. A trusted advisor, a friend who sees things differently, even a financial planner. Other people aren't free from bias either, but they're often free from *your* bias. They can ask questions you've avoided, challenge your assumptions, and help you see what your mind is trained to overlook.

Fourth, we slow down. Most cognitive biases thrive in speed. Fast decisions leave no room for reflection. If something feels urgent, it's probably not. If something feels *too* good or *too* scary, give it time. Time is clarity's greatest ally.

Finally, we embrace humility. The more certain you feel, the more cautious you should be. Certainty is often a signal—not of insight, but of blindness. A wise investor doesn't just study the market. They study themselves. They don't just ask, *What is the smartest move?* They also ask, *What is the move I am most likely to mess up?*

Biases aren't going away. They live in the very structure of how we think. But that doesn't mean we're doomed to repeat the same mistakes. With awareness, with systems, and with a healthy dose of self-doubt, we can build decision-making frameworks that help us move through the noise—not perfectly, but more clearly. And in a world where clarity is rare, that may be the greatest financial advantage of all.

Loss Aversion and the Power of Avoidance

If there is one bias that deserves a spotlight in the world of money, it is loss aversion—the deep, instinctual tendency for human beings to fear losing something far more than they desire gaining the same thing.

Psychologists Daniel Kahneman and Amos Tversky famously demonstrated this phenomenon in their research on prospect theory, showing that the emotional pain of losing $100 is significantly more intense than the pleasure of gaining $100. The takeaway wasn't just academic. It revealed something essential about human psychology: we are not wired to seek gains—we are wired to avoid loss.

At first glance, that might seem like a prudent instinct. Avoiding loss, after all, can protect us from danger. It can keep us from making reckless decisions or overextending ourselves. But when it comes to personal finance, investing, and building long-term wealth, loss aversion can quietly sabotage the very progress we're trying to make. It convinces us to stay still when we should move, to hold back when we should reach forward, and to focus so obsessively on what might go wrong that we miss everything that could go right.

Loss aversion is not just about major financial decisions—it's baked into everyday behavior. Consider the way most people feel about their possessions. Once you own something—be it a car, a house, or even a subscription service—it takes on a new kind of value. You're no longer assessing it objectively. Now, losing it feels personal. This is known as the endowment effect, and it's a direct cousin of loss aversion. You value things more simply because they are *yours*, and therefore, letting go of them feels like a loss—even if it no longer serves you or makes financial sense.

This is why so many people hold on to losing stocks or underperforming assets. It's not that they've done the math and concluded that staying is the better strategy. It's that selling would force them to *realize* the loss, to make it official, to admit defeat. As long as the loss is only on paper, they can pretend it's not real. But that illusion comes at a cost: they remain stuck in investments with no real future, their capital frozen in regret.

The same pattern appears in business. Entrepreneurs often continue pouring money and time into failing ventures, not because the fundamentals support it, but because walking away feels like losing. It's not just about the money—it's about identity. Pride. Hope. And in those moments, the logical voice that says *"cut your losses and move on"* gets drowned out by a louder, more painful whisper: *"you can't let this go—it means you failed."*

In the short term, loss aversion feels protective. It keeps you from making hasty decisions. It urges caution. But over time, it becomes a quiet thief. It steals opportunity. It convinces people to stay in low-risk, low- return investments that don't even keep up with inflation. It prevents them from switching careers, starting a business, moving to a better city, or pursuing a new life path—because each of those changes involves letting go of something familiar, and therefore, risking loss.

Even when the loss is imaginary or symbolic, the emotional response is real. Think about how many people refuse to sell an old car, even though it costs more to maintain than it's worth. Or how many cling to unused gym memberships or streaming services because "you never know." These are not logical decisions—they are emotional reactions to the fear of letting go. And in aggregate, they add up. Over years and decades, the weight of what we refuse to release becomes a burden too heavy to ignore.

In the stock market, loss aversion creates another toxic pattern: selling too early. The moment an investment begins to show a gain, many people rush to lock in the profit—not because it's the smart move, but because they're terrified of that gain disappearing. Ironically, they often hold onto their losing investments *too long* and sell their winners *too soon*. That's not strategy. That's emotion pretending to be strategy.

The tragedy of loss aversion is that it not only causes people to *act* when they shouldn't—it often causes them to *not act* when they should. It paralyzes decision-making. It feeds procrastination. It keeps people sitting on the sidelines of opportunity because they are so focused on protecting what they have that they never consider what they could build. It's the person who never invests at all, because they fear losing their initial savings. It's the employee who never negotiates for a raise because they're afraid of rocking the boat. It's the homeowner who won't downsize, even though the costs of upkeep are slowly draining them, because parting with the house feels like losing part of their identity.

And perhaps most cruelly, loss aversion can even affect people who have *already won*. Imagine someone who has built wealth over years of smart investing and disciplined saving. Instead of feeling empowered, they now live in a constant state of protection, terrified that one wrong move will cost them everything. Their focus shifts from creation to defense. They no longer take calculated risks. They no longer dream expansively. They just guard what they have, shrinking their decisions to match their growing fear.

Ironically, the wealth they once built to give them freedom becomes a prison guarded by anxiety. So how do we deal with this invisible enemy? How do we stop fear from driving our financial life?

The first step is awareness. You have to recognize the signs of loss aversion in your own behavior. Ask yourself: Am I holding onto this investment, subscription, or habit because it serves me—or because I'm afraid to lose it? Am I making decisions to move forward—or simply to avoid pain? Am I basing my strategy on potential or on protection?

The second step is to reframe loss itself. Instead of seeing it as failure, begin to view it as part of the process. Every investor takes losses. Every entrepreneur faces setbacks. Every meaningful journey requires giving something up. Losing is not the opposite of progress—it's a prerequisite for it. The more you normalize loss, the less power it holds over you. You begin to see that losing money isn't the worst thing that can happen. Staying stuck might be.

You can also reduce the sting of loss by creating systems that separate emotion from action. For example, using a dollar-cost averaging strategy in investing removes the temptation to buy or sell based on short- term emotions. Automating your savings or budgeting according to rules you set in advance takes the pressure off in-the-moment decisions. Pre-committing to certain behaviors creates a buffer between you and the panic that loss often triggers.

Perspective matters, too. Zooming out helps soften the sharp edge of temporary setbacks. If your investment portfolio drops 10% in a week, it might feel catastrophic—until you remember that your time horizon is thirty years. If you lose money trying something new, it might hurt—until you remember that the alternative was stagnation. The broader your perspective, the smaller each loss becomes.

One of the most powerful tools in managing loss aversion is gratitude. That might sound strange in a chapter about money, but gratitude shifts your focus from what you *might lose* to what you *already have*. When you're rooted in enoughness, when you're anchored in what's working, loss becomes less threatening. It no longer feels like the end of the world—it's just part of the dance.

You can also practice what's known as "pre-mortem thinking"—an exercise where you imagine that your decision has failed, and you explore *why*. This isn't pessimism. It's preparation. It helps you identify risks in advance and plan accordingly. Ironically, by confronting loss head-on, you reduce its power. It becomes familiar, manageable, even navigable.

Finally, remember that money is not just math—it's meaning. Loss only feels devastating when it attacks your identity. If you tie your self-worth to your bank account, then any financial dip feels like a personal insult. But if you see money as a tool, not a mirror, then losses become feedback, not judgment. They don't define you. They inform you.

Loss aversion is powerful, yes. But it's not destiny. You are allowed to care about what you've built. You are allowed to protect what matters. But when protection becomes paralysis, when safety becomes your prison, when avoiding discomfort becomes your strategy—then it's time to look deeper.

Because the truth is this: you will lose money. You will make mistakes. You will take risks that don't pan out. And that's okay. It means you're in the game. It means you're alive. It means you're trying.

And in the end, it's not the losses that shape your financial future. It's how you respond to them. It's the bounce. The lesson. The choice to keep going.

Confirmation Bias and the Echo Chamber Effect

We like to think that we are open-minded. That when faced with new information, we evaluate it fairly, weigh the evidence, and adjust our views accordingly. That we are capable of changing our minds when truth demands it. But in reality, most of us don't seek truth—we seek *comfort*. And there is no greater source of psychological comfort than validation. This is the essence of confirmation bias: the tendency to interpret, favor, and recall information that confirms what we already believe, while ignoring or dismissing anything that challenges our assumptions.

In the world of money, this bias is not just common—it's costly. Financial decisions, by their very nature, involve uncertainty. And in uncertain environments, we crave a sense of control. Confirmation bias gives us that illusion. It wraps us in the safety of our own opinions, reinforced by selectively chosen data, selectively heard advice, and selectively remembered experiences. It creates an echo chamber around our beliefs—an invisible room where every voice agrees with us, not because they're right, but because we've filtered out everything that doesn't align.

Imagine an investor who believes that cryptocurrency is the future. They follow influencers who support that belief. They subscribe to newsletters that celebrate every upward spike. They ignore the warnings, skip the articles that suggest regulation might change the game, and dismiss anyone who questions long-term viability as a dinosaur or a cynic. They don't just believe—they build an entire reality that feeds that belief, every day.

Or take someone who's convinced that the housing market is about to crash. They scroll through headlines that reinforce that fear. They ignore data that shows price stability. They talk to people who agree. Every piece of contradictory evidence is explained away. Every uncertainty becomes another sign of the coming collapse. They think they're being cautious. But really, they're building a cage—and calling it wisdom.

The echo chamber effect created by confirmation bias is especially dangerous in the digital age. Algorithms are designed to show us more of what we already engage with. If you click on a video about gold being the only safe asset, your feed will soon be filled with the same message, over and over. It will *feel* like consensus. It will *feel* like truth. But it's not—it's simply repetition.

The more you see the same idea echoed back to you, the more you believe it's universal. This phenomenon is known as the "illusory truth effect"—the psychological tendency to believe something is true simply because you've heard it many times. In finance, this leads to bubbles. Herd mentality. Irrational exuberance. It convinces people to chase trends long after the fundamentals no longer support them.

Confirmation bias also clouds how we evaluate our own past decisions. If an investment worked out, we attribute it to insight, not luck. If it failed, we explain it away as bad timing or external forces. We rarely look at our past mistakes as signals of flawed thinking. We rewrite the story to preserve the illusion that we were right all along. This keeps us from growing. From learning. From becoming better stewards of our own resources.

But perhaps the most dangerous aspect of confirmation bias is that it doesn't just distort our thinking—it distorts our identity. We become attached to being "a certain kind of person"—the one who only buys index funds, or never carries debt, or always bets on real estate. These identities are not just financial strategies. They become *moral positions*. And once that happens, changing your mind feels like betraying yourself.

The truth is, being wrong about money isn't a character flaw. It's a learning opportunity. But confirmation bias turns it into a threat. It makes disagreement feel like an attack. It turns opposing viewpoints into enemies. It replaces curiosity with defensiveness. And in doing so, it cuts off the very path that leads to financial maturity.

So how do we break out?

The first and most powerful antidote is humility. Begin with the assumption that you are biased. That your perspective is incomplete. That your experience, no matter how rich, does not contain the whole picture.

Humility creates space for truth. It quiets the need to be right and opens the door to being better.

Second, seek out disagreement. Not to argue, but to understand. Follow people who think differently. Read articles that challenge your view. When you feel resistance rise, pause. Ask yourself: *What if they're right? What am I missing?* You don't have to change your mind—but you do have to let new information in. Growth doesn't happen in agreement. It happens in friction.

Third, track your decisions. Write down your financial choices and the reasons behind them. Include what you believe will happen and why. Then, revisit those notes in six months, or a year. Were you right? Was your reasoning sound? This practice, known as a "decision journal," exposes patterns. It reveals whether your logic is consistent or if your memory has been revised to protect your ego.

Fourth, invite outside feedback. Talk to a mentor, a planner, or a friend who isn't afraid to challenge you. Ask them to play devil's advocate. Listen. Don't defend—just listen. Often, a single outside voice can shatter the illusion you've built around a faulty belief.

Fifth, learn to separate *belief* from *behavior*. It's okay to have a thesis, an opinion, a framework. But make sure your actions are based on evidence, not ideology. If your belief says "never borrow money," but the math says a low-interest loan makes sense for a specific investment, be willing to adjust. Dogma is not a strategy.

Finally, remember that changing your mind is not weakness—it's evolution. Every wise investor, every successful entrepreneur, every financially resilient person you admire has changed their mind—often. They have updated their beliefs, refined their models, and pivoted when reality demanded it. That's not flip- flopping. That's progress.

Confirmation bias will never fully disappear. It's part of the human experience. But awareness reduces its grip. When you recognize the echo chamber forming around your financial life, you can step outside of it. You can walk toward the discomfort of opposing ideas. You can sit in the tension between certainty and possibility.

And in that space—where humility meets curiosity—you begin to see more clearly. You begin to think more freely. And you give yourself the greatest financial advantage of all: the ability to *change* when it matters most.

Building a Better Decision Filter

Every financial decision you make—whether it's buying a house, choosing an investment strategy, switching jobs, or simply deciding whether to splurge or save—passes through a kind of internal filter. That filter is shaped by your emotions, beliefs, experiences, and mental shortcuts. The quality of that filter determines the quality of your decisions. And if the previous chapters have shown us anything, it's that most of us are using filters that are—at best—clogged with bias, and—at worst—actively working against us.

If we want to become better with money—not just smarter, but wiser—we don't necessarily need more data. We need a better way of deciding. A better way of thinking. A cleaner, more intentional decision filter that helps us navigate complexity without getting lost in emotion, ego, or illusion.

The first step to building this better filter is understanding that *clarity is a skill*. It's not something you either have or don't have. It's something you practice. And like all skills, it starts with slowing down. One of the most dangerous financial patterns is speed—rushed decisions made in moments of stress, urgency, or euphoria. When you move too fast, you default to instinct. And as we've seen, instinct is often just a reflection of your deepest, least-examined biases.

So slow down. When faced with a major financial choice, give yourself time. Create a 24-hour or even 72- hour rule for big purchases or investments. Let the initial emotional wave pass. Often, what feels urgent today will look very different tomorrow. This pause is not hesitation—it's power. It creates space for logic to re-enter the conversation.

The second component of a strong decision filter is *intentional questioning*. Before making a financial move, ask yourself:

- What problem am I actually trying to solve? • What am I afraid of losing?

- What would I advise a friend to do in the same situation? • Is this based on facts—or feelings?

- Will this decision serve me five years from now?

These questions might seem basic, even obvious. But in moments of pressure, we rarely ask them. We react. We assume. We follow the crowd or our gut. But a good decision filter doesn't assume—it interrogates. It asks better questions so you can make better choices.

Next, consider building *rules* into your financial life. Rules protect you from yourself. They turn intention into structure. For example: "I only invest in assets I understand." Or: "I save 20% of every paycheck, no matter what." Or: "I never make a financial decision when I'm angry, excited, or scared." These rules act as pre-commitments. They remove ambiguity. They reduce the influence of momentary emotions.

Think of these rules as the *guardrails* of your financial road. They won't make every decision for you, but they'll keep you from veering off the cliff.

Another critical element in refining your decision filter is *perspective shifting*. Financial decisions often feel overwhelming because we view them through a narrow lens—today's problems, this week's bills, this year's economy. But wise decision-makers think in decades. They zoom out. They ask: *How does this fit into the bigger picture of my life?*

If you're considering taking a new job that pays more but will drain your energy and cost you time with your family, the question isn't just "How much money will I make?" It's "What kind of life will this create for me?" If you're tempted to invest in a volatile asset, the question isn't "Can I make a quick gain?" It's "Will this support my long-term goals—or just feed my short-term ego?"

This long-view thinking doesn't eliminate risk, but it puts risk in context. It reminds you that the goal isn't just to win today. It's to keep winning, over time.

To that end, your decision filter should also include *post-analysis*. Most people make decisions and then move on. But reflection is where learning happens. After every significant financial choice—whether it went well or poorly—ask:

- What worked? • What didn't?

- What did I miss?

- What can I do differently next time?

This kind of reflection is rare, but it's what separates amateurs from pros. It helps you refine your process, not just your outcome. Over time, you stop guessing. You start seeing patterns. You build a personal financial philosophy grounded in lived experience—not just internet advice.

A powerful addition to your filter is *mental modeling*. This means borrowing frameworks from other disciplines to guide your thinking. For instance, you might use **inversion**: instead of asking "How can I build wealth?", ask "What could cause me to lose everything?" and avoid those behaviors. Or **second-order thinking**: instead of asking "What happens if I do this?", ask "What happens next, and then next, and then next?" The more levels of consequence you consider, the clearer your choice becomes.

Equally important is your *emotional awareness*. Emotions aren't the enemy of good decisions—but unexamined emotions are. Start tuning into how you *feel* when you make financial choices. Are you anxious? Overconfident? Desperate? Euphoric? Each emotion carries a message. Learn to hear it, not obey it blindly.

Sometimes, the best decision is to do nothing. To wait. To let the fog clear. Other times, the best decision is to leap—despite the fear. A good decision filter doesn't eliminate emotion. It holds it in balance. It acknowledges your feelings while still honoring your goals.

One overlooked part of decision filtering is *values alignment*. Often, we make financially smart decisions that feel wrong in hindsight—not because the math was off, but because the choice violated something deeper. A core value. A priority. A personal principle. Your best financial life will not be built on profit alone. It will be built on choices that reflect who you are and what you care about.

Before making a big decision, ask: *Does this support the kind of life I want to live? Does it reflect the person I'm trying to become?* Sometimes, the "right" financial decision on paper is the wrong one in your soul.

Don't ignore that voice.

Finally, surround yourself with *better inputs*. Your decisions are only as good as the information that feeds them. Seek diverse perspectives. Learn from people who think differently. Question experts. Read broadly. Follow contrarian thinkers as well as mainstream voices. A strong decision filter is not a bubble—it's a gate. It keeps out noise while letting in truth.

Building this kind of decision-making framework takes time. It's not a weekend project. It's a lifelong practice. You will still make mistakes. You will still get things wrong. But over time, your misses will become less frequent, less costly, and more educational.

You'll stop relying on guesses and gut reactions. You'll begin to trust your process. And when you do, you'll discover something powerful: peace. Not because you've eliminated uncertainty—but because you've created clarity in the face of it.

That is the true goal of financial intelligence. Not perfection. Not omniscience. But *clarity*. The quiet confidence that comes from knowing that no matter what happens next, you've built a decision filter strong enough to face it with both wisdom and grace.

Chapter 6: Patience Pays—But Few Wait

We live in an age of now. Of instant messages, next-day delivery, five-minute workouts, same-day trades, and swipe-right relationships. Everything around us is designed to compress time—to eliminate waiting, to shrink the gap between desire and satisfaction, to deliver results not just quickly but *immediately*. And in many ways, it's remarkable. Convenience has liberated us from endless inefficiencies. It has made life faster, lighter, more connected. But in the realm of money, this cultural addiction to immediacy has come at a cost—one that is invisible to the impatient eye.

Because wealth—the real kind, the kind that endures—does not operate on a fast-forward button. It is not built in sprints, but in marathons. It doesn't reward clever timing or quick exits. It honors patience. And patience, in the world of finance, is not just a virtue—it's a strategy. Perhaps the most powerful one of all.

But here's the dilemma: patience isn't natural to us.

As human beings, we are biologically wired for immediacy. Our ancestors were not concerned with 30-year returns—they were concerned with surviving the next 30 minutes. Our brains evolved to prioritize quick wins, short-term threats, immediate resources. In evolutionary terms, long-term planning was a luxury most couldn't afford. And even though the world has changed, our wiring has not. That's why the thrill of a sudden windfall still floods us with dopamine. That's why checking our investment apps five times a day feels important. That's why we sell too soon, panic too early, and abandon the long game for short-term certainty.

Patience, in this context, is not passive. It's not about waiting around and hoping things work out. It is *active resistance* to a world that demands urgency. It's a daily decision to zoom out, to delay gratification, to stay still while others chase. It's not glamorous. It's not exciting. But it is *profitable*—over time.

And that's the caveat most people miss: *over time*. Patience doesn't always feel rewarding in the moment. In fact, it often feels like you're being left behind. Like everyone else is getting rich faster. Like your slow, steady, boring approach is for fools. That's because the benefits of patience are invisible until they aren't. They compound quietly, below the surface, like seeds germinating underground. And then, one day, seemingly all at once, the harvest appears. But the work was done long before the reward.

This delayed visibility is why patience is so underappreciated. You don't get praise for holding an investment for ten years. You don't go viral for steadily saving a portion of your income each month. You don't get applause for *not* selling during a downturn. But these are the behaviors that build real wealth.

They are unsexy. Uncelebrated. And unbelievably effective.

Look at the lives of the wealthiest individuals who built their fortunes over time—not those who inherited or stumbled into sudden success, but those who *built*. Warren Buffett, for example, is not rich simply because he's a brilliant investor—he's rich because he started early and *never stopped*. He allowed time, not timing, to do the heavy lifting. The majority of his net worth came after his 60th birthday, not because his strategy changed, but because time finally revealed its reward.

This truth runs counter to the financial media's obsession with urgency. Headlines scream about market crashes, once-in-a-lifetime opportunities, and urgent moves you "must" make today. But most wealth isn't made in reaction to headlines. It's made by tuning them out. By focusing not on what's happening this week, but on what you're building this decade.

Impatience makes you reactive. It leads to buying high and selling low. It convinces you that volatility is risk, rather than opportunity. It pushes you to compare your journey to others, to benchmark your progress against artificial timelines. But money is not a race. It's not about keeping up. It's about staying in.

Staying in—despite boredom, doubt, fear, and external noise—is hard. That's why patience is rare. And that rarity is precisely what makes it so valuable.

Because when everyone else is chasing the next big thing, the patient person is quietly growing something that lasts. While others are gambling on trends, the patient person is compounding consistency. And while others burn out or break down, the patient person endures. That endurance is the edge.

Patience also allows for better decision-making. It gives you space to evaluate rather than react. To understand cycles. To see beyond the emotion of the moment. Markets rise and fall. Trends come and go. But the patient person isn't thrown off course. They've anchored their strategy in time, not timing. They've chosen a pace they can sustain, not a sprint they can't.

But patience doesn't mean inaction. It's not about sitting still forever. It means acting deliberately, based on principles, not panic. It means investing when others are afraid, and staying invested when others are restless. It means saving steadily even when it feels like nothing is happening. It means building systems you trust and letting those systems run—without micromanaging every blip on the radar.

It also means being patient not just with results—but with *yourself*. Financial success is not linear. There will be missteps, moments of fear, times when you wonder if you're doing it wrong. Patience allows grace. It lets you keep going without needing perfection. It lets you hold the long view even when the short-term feels shaky.

This applies not only to investing, but to career building, entrepreneurship, debt reduction, and lifestyle design. The slow route is often the most sustainable one. It gives you room to breathe. To learn. To grow into your goals. The person who builds gradually builds *resilience* alongside wealth. And resilience is the real safety net—not just a number in a bank account, but the confidence that comes from knowing you can endure.

The irony of patience is that while it feels like you're delaying gratification, what you're really doing is *multiplying* it. Not just financially, but emotionally. Because the kind of peace, stability, and freedom that come from long-term thinking are not available to the impatient. They belong to those who can wait. Who can build in silence. Who can trust the process.

But that trust must be built intentionally. It doesn't come naturally. It comes from knowing your plan, from understanding the math of compounding, from studying history and seeing how time has always rewarded discipline. It comes from choosing principles over impulses, and process over perfection.

In the chapters that follow, we'll explore why we're wired for quick wins (6.1), how compounding works its quiet magic (6.2), why "time in the market" beats "timing the market" every single time (6.3), how delayed gratification becomes a modern-day superpower (6.4), and finally, how to train your mind to think in decades, not days (6.5).

Because if there's one truth that echoes across every wealth journey worth studying, it's this:

The ones who win aren't the fastest. They're the ones who don't quit.

Why We're Wired for Instant Results

Somewhere deep inside your brain—beneath the logic, beyond the goals and spreadsheets and carefully calculated financial strategies—there is a very old voice. It whispers things like, "Now. Quick. Grab it before it's gone." It speaks the language of instinct, not reason. And it's not concerned with your five-year plan or your retirement account. It's concerned with survival. And from its perspective, patience is a risk. Waiting is dangerous. And long-term thinking is a luxury only afforded by those who forget what it once meant to live hand-to-mouth.

This ancient voice is not a flaw. It's part of you. It's evolutionary design. And it shapes your relationship with money far more than most people realize.

Let's go back tens of thousands of years, to a time when humans were not investors or strategists or entrepreneurs. We were hunters. Foragers. Survivalists living in immediate reality. If we found food, we ate it. If we saw danger, we ran. If we needed shelter, we built it fast. The concept of saving—of setting something aside for the future—only existed in the most rudimentary forms. There were no retirement accounts. No stock markets. No interest rates. Only now. This hour. This night.

In such a world, patience wasn't just unnecessary—it could be fatal. Waiting for the "right time" to eat might mean starving. Waiting to act could mean being eaten. Our nervous systems were designed for rapid response, quick reward, and immediate feedback. And though we've traded caves for condos and spears for smartphones, our biology hasn't updated to match the modern world.

That's why, today, even with all our education and access to information, we still feel a jolt of satisfaction when a package arrives the same day. Or when our investments spike overnight. Or when we make a financial decision that delivers immediate gratification, even if it compromises our long-term goals. That jolt is dopamine. It's the same neurochemical our ancestors got from securing a fresh kill or finding ripe fruit. It feels like victory. Like safety. Like control.

And this is precisely the challenge: our emotional circuitry is optimized for short-term wins in a long-term game.

Modern finance, unlike the world we evolved in, punishes impatience. It rewards endurance, not speed. It favors those who can delay gratification, ignore noise, and stay the course when everything screams for action. But because our biology is still tuned to the now, we constantly feel pulled toward behaviors that sabotage our financial wellbeing.

Think about how we consume news: every headline is urgent, every update framed as critical. You're told the market just moved. A new IPO is coming. Inflation is rising. Rates are falling. Click. React. Decide. Now. This constant stimulation activates the same parts of our brain once used for scanning the horizon for predators. The difference? Back then, it was about staying alive. Today, it's about staying informed—at the cost of our peace and patience.

This phenomenon is amplified by modern technology. Apps designed to reward you with flashy graphics when you trade. Notifications engineered to hijack your attention. Social media feeds that glorify overnight success and compare your journey to someone else's highlight reel. These tools were built not to educate you—but to *engage* you. And engagement, in a world ruled by attention economies, is best achieved through urgency and impulse.

It's no wonder, then, that we struggle to wait.

Waiting feels like doing nothing. And doing nothing, in a world that praises hustle and hustle culture, feels like failure. But here's the paradox: in finance, some of the most successful decisions are not actions— they're inactions. Holding through a downturn. Saying no to a flashy opportunity. Resisting the urge to tinker with a strategy that already works. These don't feel like accomplishments. But they are. In fact, they're some of the hardest accomplishments you'll ever achieve.

Why? Because they go against your wiring.

This is why patience must be trained. It must be treated not as a default trait, but as a *skill*—one that requires conscious practice, reinforcement, and protection.

Start with awareness. Recognize when your biology is hijacking your behavior. Notice the temptation to act quickly. Ask yourself: "Is this urgency real—or just familiar?" Many of our financial mistakes come not from poor logic, but from poor emotional management. We panic. We chase. We fear missing out. And so we act—not because it's smart, but because it feels safer than sitting still.

Next, build systems that slow you down. Set time-based rules for decision-making. For example: "I don't sell anything unless I've held it for a year," or "I wait 48 hours before making any major financial choice." These rules act like circuit breakers. They interrupt your default impulses and give your rational mind time to catch up.

Another powerful tool is reframing. Instead of seeing waiting as passive, see it as *active alignment*. You are not "doing nothing." You are aligning your present behavior with your future goals. You are resisting the gravity of now to protect the vision of later. That's not weak—it's powerful.

Visualization helps here. Picture the version of yourself five years from now. What did they need you to do today? Often, they don't need you to make a brilliant move. They need you to *not* make a destructive one. They need you to keep saving. Keep investing. Keep showing up for your plan, even when results aren't instant.

Delayed gratification—the ability to resist a smaller reward now for a greater one later—is one of the most consistent predictors of long-term financial success. But it doesn't come naturally. It must be cultivated.

One way to build it is by celebrating process over outcome. Most of us only celebrate when the portfolio goes up, when the goal is hit, when the result is visible. But this reinforces the need for quick results.

Instead, start celebrating the *habit*. The deposit you made. The decision you delayed. The temptation you resisted. These are wins, too—arguably the most important ones.

Your environment matters, too. Surround yourself with voices, people, and philosophies that reinforce long-term thinking. If you're constantly consuming content that glorifies speed, hacks, and rapid gains, you will internalize those values—even unconsciously. Choose your financial influences carefully. Curate your inputs with the same discipline you apply to your outputs.

Lastly, be kind to yourself. This work is hard. You are not weak for feeling impatient. You are human. The goal is not to eliminate your impulses, but to understand them. To meet them with curiosity, not shame.

Every time you feel the urge to act prematurely and *choose not to*, you are rewiring your brain. You are strengthening your patience muscle.

And that muscle, over time, will give you an edge that few possess.

Because while others are scrambling for quick gains, chasing trends, and burning out on the treadmill of urgency, you will be steady. You will be growing—not in bursts, but in layers. Not in noise, but in silence. And one day, when the compound effects of your patient decisions begin to reveal themselves, people will ask how you did it.

And you'll smile. Because you'll know that the answer isn't a secret or a shortcut. It's a simple truth few are willing to live:

The real rewards go to those who can wait.

The Misunderstood Magic of Compounding

If patience is the soil in which wealth grows, then compounding is the sunlight, water, and time that turn a single seed into a forest. It's a quiet force—one that moves in near silence, almost imperceptibly at first, then shockingly fast. It works like gravity in reverse, drawing small choices upward into exponential returns. And yet, despite its immense power, compounding remains one of the most misunderstood principles in all of finance.

Most people hear the word and think of it in purely mathematical terms—interest on interest, growth on growth. They picture charts with gentle curves that turn sharply upward toward the end. But compounding is not just about numbers. It's about behavior. Belief. Discipline. It's not just a formula—it's a philosophy. And embracing it requires a mindset shift so profound that, for many, it borders on spiritual.

Let's begin with the basics, the part we all learned in school but few of us truly absorbed. When you invest money, that money earns returns. If you reinvest those returns, then *they*, too, begin to earn returns. This creates a snowball effect, where your money begins to grow not in a straight line, but in a curve—a curve that steepens dramatically the longer you let it roll. It's not the amount you invest or even the rate of return that makes the biggest difference—it's *how long* you allow the process to continue uninterrupted.

Consider two investors. One starts at age 20, saves diligently for 10 years, then stops. The other waits until 30, but invests the same amount every year until retirement. Who ends up with more? In many cases, it's the first investor—*not* because they saved more, but because they started earlier. The magic wasn't in the dollars; it was in the *decades*. The difference wasn't the effort, but the time.

And that's where the misunderstanding begins. Because compounding doesn't reward intensity. It rewards consistency. It doesn't care how smart you are, how aggressive you are, or how perfectly you time the market. It cares how long you can stay in the game without interrupting the process.

But in a culture obsessed with speed, waiting is hard. The early years of compounding feel unrewarding. The gains are small. The curve is flat. You look at your account and wonder if it's even working.

Meanwhile, someone else just doubled their money with a lucky trade. Another person just bought crypto and made headlines. A third person seems to be sprinting toward wealth while you crawl. And the temptation to abandon compounding for something more *exciting* grows stronger.

This is where most people go wrong—not because they don't understand the math, but because they underestimate the *emotional discipline* compounding requires.

Compounding is boring—until it's breathtaking. It's invisible—until it's undeniable. And that delayed payoff tests our patience, our resolve, and our ability to stay the course while others chase faster results. It asks you to be okay with small progress, to trust a process that offers no immediate validation, to keep showing up without applause or reassurance.

Think about how we approach health, learning, or relationships. The same principle applies. Going to the gym once changes nothing. Reading a single book won't make you wise. Having one honest conversation won't transform a relationship. But doing these things consistently over time? That changes everything.

Compounding isn't unique to finance—it's a universal law of growth. Small actions, multiplied by time, lead to extraordinary outcomes.

So why do so many people abandon it?

Because compounding is fragile. It breaks easily. One interruption—an impulsive decision, a panic sale, a loss of faith—and the snowball stops rolling. You don't just lose momentum; you lose *trajectory*. That's why the true challenge of compounding isn't understanding how it works—it's protecting it. It's resisting the urge to meddle, to "optimize," to chase novelty. It's learning to value *stillness* in a world that prizes constant motion.

There's also a more subtle misunderstanding: many people see compounding as something that happens *to* their money. But the most powerful compounding doesn't happen in your bank account—it happens in your *behavior*.

Every time you make a smart financial decision—no matter how small—you reinforce your identity as someone who's responsible, strategic, and long-term oriented. That identity compounds. It makes the next smart choice easier. And the next. Over time, you're not just growing wealth—you're growing *wisdom*.

You're training your mind to value the future more than the moment. You're shifting from reactive to intentional. From fragile to resilient.

Your habits, too, compound. Save a little more this month. Learn a new skill. Cut one recurring expense. These actions seem insignificant in isolation. But repeated, they create a financial foundation far stronger than any market return could offer. You're not just investing money—you're investing in *yourself*. And that investment pays the highest compound interest of all.

Now, let's talk about the flip side: compounding doesn't just work in your favor. It can work against you.

Debt compounds. Bad habits compound. Delayed decisions compound. Every time you avoid facing your finances, ignore your budget, or let fear dictate your actions, the consequences accumulate. Slowly at first. Then sharply. Just like positive growth, negative patterns accelerate with time.

That's why financial self-awareness is critical. You must know not only where your money is growing—but where it's silently leaking. And just as you would nurture the positive snowball, you must stop the negative one before it gains speed.

Another overlooked truth: compounding works best when it's *left alone*. The most powerful investors often look passive—not because they are lazy, but because they've learned that overmanaging can be a liability. Every time you jump in to tweak, adjust, or "fix" your portfolio, you risk breaking the compounding engine.

Warren Buffett is famously quoted as saying, "The stock market is a device for transferring money from the impatient to the patient." But it's also a mirror. It reflects our character, our temperament, our ability to trust what we can't yet see.

Because here's the ultimate irony: the more you chase quick growth, the less likely you are to experience exponential returns. The more you fiddle, the more you fracture your progress. The most powerful growth is often the *quietest*. The most life-changing wealth is usually built in the *shadows* of consistent, patient, intentional behavior.

Compounding also teaches us a deeper lesson about time itself. In a world that treats time like a threat—as something to beat, race against, or escape—compounding reframes it as your greatest ally. Every day you wait, every month you stay invested, every year you resist interruption, time works harder for you. It's not your enemy—it's your leverage.

So how do you truly embrace compounding?

First, you automate as much as possible. Automate your savings. Your investments. Your debt payments. Remove emotion from the equation. Let your systems protect you from your impulses.

Second, you monitor less, not more. Checking your accounts daily does nothing for your results and everything for your anxiety. Compounding works best when you give it space.

Third, you celebrate time, not timing. You don't need to be perfect. You just need to *not quit*. If you missed the best day in the market—don't worry. Stay in. Time has more days to give.

Fourth, you zoom out. Focus less on what happened this week or month, and more on what you're building this decade. Ask: "Will this decision still serve me in ten years?"

And finally, you stay humble. Compounding rewards those who don't try to outsmart it. Who respect the curve. Who play the long game not because it's trendy, but because it's *true*.

In the end, compounding is less about finance and more about faith. Faith in time. Faith in small beginnings. Faith that what feels slow is often secretly powerful. And that what looks like nothing is often becoming something—quietly, steadily, undeniably.

Because wealth, like wisdom, does not come in waves.

It comes in ripples—until one day, the ripples become a tide.

Time in the Market Beats Timing the Market

Every investor, at some point, dreams of catching the perfect moment—buying just before a massive market rally or selling seconds before a sharp crash. It's the allure of market timing: the idea that if you're smart enough, fast enough, or connected enough, you can outmaneuver everyone else and leapfrog your way to wealth. It's the fantasy of winning the financial game by predicting what happens next.

But here's the sobering truth: almost no one can do it consistently. Not the average investor. Not most professionals. Not even many hedge fund managers with armies of analysts and algorithms behind them. Why? Because timing the market isn't just hard—it's almost impossible. And the cost of getting it wrong, even slightly, is enormous.

That's why, in the long run, the people who build the most wealth aren't the ones who jump in and out with perfect precision. They're the ones who stay in. Who weather the storms. Who ride the cycles. Who plant their investments like seeds and let time—not tactics—do the heavy lifting. Let's break this down.

Markets are emotional organisms. They don't move in straight lines. They swing between fear and greed, between euphoria and panic. And those swings are impossible to predict with accuracy over the long term. Yes, you might get lucky once. You might even get lucky twice. But eventually, the odds catch up. Because markets don't just test your intellect—they test your *temperament*. And temperament is far more important than timing.

Consider this example: Over a 20-year period, if you had been fully invested in the market and just let your money sit, you would've captured all the growth those decades offered. But if you missed just the *10 best days*—yes, only 10—you would've lost a significant portion of your total returns. The best days often come *right after* the worst ones, which means if you bailed out during a downturn, you likely missed the rebound. And missing the rebound is what devastates returns—not staying in through the dip.

This isn't theory. It's math. And the math is merciless.

Yet people still try to time the market. Why? Because it *feels* safer. Selling during uncertainty creates the illusion of control. You tell yourself, "I'll just wait for things to settle down," or "I'll jump back in when it looks better." But the market doesn't send invitations. It doesn't say, "Hey, today's the bottom. Feel free to invest now." The turning points only become clear in hindsight. And by then, the gains are already gone.

Timing the market also triggers emotional whiplash. It turns investing into a series of high-stakes decisions: When to enter? When to exit? Is this the dip—or the start of a crash? This creates anxiety, decision fatigue, and second-guessing. You're no longer investing—you're gambling. Not with dice, but with your peace of mind.

Now contrast that with staying in the market. Not constantly tweaking. Not chasing news. Just building a solid, diversified portfolio and letting time work. It's less exciting. Less dramatic. But infinitely more effective.

Think of the market like a wild ocean. Some days it's calm. Some days it's violent. If you try to surf every wave, you'll wipe out. But if you anchor a boat and stay put—yes, you'll get tossed around—but you'll also remain afloat, long enough to reach the other shore. That's what time in the market does: it anchors you through chaos. It absorbs the volatility. It transforms randomness into returns.

Because despite the daily drama, the long-term trend of the market—especially broad, diversified markets

—is upward. Over decades, economies grow. Companies innovate. Populations expand. Productivity increases. And those forces drive stock prices higher over time. Not every year. Not every month. But over the arc of decades, the market rewards participation.

Let's also talk about the cost of missing opportunities—not just by getting out too early, but by waiting too long to start.

Many people delay investing because they're waiting for "the right time." They tell themselves, "I'll start when the market dips," or "after the election," or "when things feel more stable." But perfect clarity never arrives. There's always uncertainty. Always noise. Always something to fear. And while you're waiting, the most valuable asset you have—*time*—is slipping away.

Remember: compound growth is exponential. The earlier you start, the less you need to contribute. Time does the heavy lifting. Waiting even a few years can mean the difference between financial freedom and forever playing catch-up. The irony? Most people delay because they think waiting is safer. But in reality, it's the *most expensive* decision you can make.

This is why consistent investing—even in imperfect times—beats perfect timing. Dollar-cost averaging, for example, is a simple strategy where you invest a fixed amount regularly, regardless of market conditions.

Some months you buy high. Some months you buy low. But over time, the highs and lows average out, and you remove emotion from the equation. It's boring. Predictable. And incredibly effective.

Here's another hidden truth: staying in the market is a bet—not on a specific company or sector, but on human progress. On innovation. On creativity. On resilience. Every time you invest and hold, you are saying, "I believe we will continue to build, adapt, and grow." That belief has been rewarded time and time again. Through wars, recessions, pandemics, crashes—the long-term trend has held. Because human progress, though uneven and unpredictable, is relentless.

Now, let's be clear: staying in the market doesn't mean ignoring risk. It means understanding it. It means building a diversified portfolio, aligned with your goals and time horizon. It means preparing emotionally for downturns, knowing they are *normal*—not signs of failure. It means playing offense *and* defense, not by trying to time exits, but by ensuring your strategy can withstand storms.

Some people worry that "buy and hold" is too passive. But real patience is active. It takes strength to watch the market dip and do nothing. It takes discipline to stick to your plan when everyone else is panicking. It takes wisdom to trust a process that offers no instant validation.

And let's not forget: time in the market doesn't just protect you from losses—it creates *compounding*. The longer you stay invested, the more your gains generate their own gains. And those gains generate more. It's a snowball effect that accelerates not in months, but in *decades*.

Trying to time the market, on the other hand, interrupts this process. It breaks the snowball. Every sale is a reset. Every re-entry comes with uncertainty. You don't just lose potential gains—you lose *momentum*.

And momentum is everything. So what does this mean for you?

It means stop obsessing over entry points. Start now. Invest consistently. And focus on time in the market, not perfect timing. Build a portfolio you believe in—and then believe in your portfolio.

It means stop comparing your journey to someone else's. They might have had a lucky break. Or a risky bet that paid off. That doesn't mean their strategy is better—it just means it hasn't broken *yet*. Sustainable wealth isn't built on gambling. It's built on enduring.

It means stop fearing every dip. The market has always recovered. Not because of blind optimism, but because economies are dynamic, and humans are resilient. Bet on that.

It means educate yourself—not on timing tricks or short-term predictions—but on *yourself*. Your goals. Your risk tolerance. Your emotional triggers. The better you know your own psychology, the more immune you become to market noise.

And finally, it means redefine what success looks like. Not as winning every month. Not as beating the market every year. But as staying in, sticking to your plan, and letting time do what it always does— reward the ones who didn't blink.

Because in the end, the market doesn't need you to be perfect. It just needs you to be present.

Delayed Gratification as a Superpower

Imagine a child sitting at a table, staring at a single marshmallow. The adult across from them offers a deal: if the child can wait fifteen minutes without eating it, they'll get a second one. The child fidgets. Some take a bite almost immediately. Others hold out for a while, then cave. But a few—just a few—wait. They resist. They endure. And when the fifteen minutes pass, they're rewarded not just with an extra marshmallow, but with something far more powerful: the proof that patience, though uncomfortable, pays.

This simple experiment, conducted in the 1960s and now famous across psychology, revealed something profound. The ability to delay gratification—to resist short-term temptation for a greater long-term reward—isn't just a sign of maturity. It's one of the strongest predictors of life success, across academics, health, relationships, and yes—money.

But here's what makes delayed gratification a true *superpower* in today's world: almost no one uses it.

We live in a culture of immediacy. One-click ordering. Instant downloads. Same-day delivery. Our technology has trained us to expect speed, convenience, and rapid feedback. Waiting, in this context, feels not just inconvenient—it feels wrong. Why delay when you can have it now? Why wait when the world is built to satisfy instantly?

Because—and this is the paradox—the most meaningful rewards in life still come slowly.

Wealth. Wisdom. Trust. Health. Mastery. These things cannot be rushed. They are the product of sustained effort, repeated action, and the willingness to resist the quick in service of the *right*. And in the realm of money, this truth becomes painfully clear.

When you spend impulsively, you get a burst of pleasure—but a long-term dent in your financial health. When you invest consistently, you may feel like nothing is happening—but years later, you have something most people never reach: stability, options, and freedom. One feels good *now*. The other feels good *forever*.

Delayed gratification flips the script. It invites you to ask not, "What will make me happy today?" but "What will serve me best five years from now?" It demands vision, restraint, and belief in a future self that you cannot yet see, but that you care enough to protect.

But let's be honest: it's hard. Resisting pleasure goes against human nature. Our brains are wired for reward, not reflection. Dopamine—the neurotransmitter of desire—floods us not when we receive something, but when we *anticipate* it. This means that even the *idea* of getting something quickly excites us. And marketing knows this. Every advertisement is designed to shortcut your thinking and spike your wanting. You don't compare, plan, or evaluate—you *react*.

And so, building the muscle of delayed gratification is not about suppressing desire. It's about training your response to it. It's about creating space between impulse and action. It's about pausing, asking, "Is this aligned with my larger goal?" and choosing long-term satisfaction over short-term escape.

One of the most powerful ways to strengthen this muscle is through *small daily decisions*. Saving instead of spending. Cooking instead of ordering out. Reading instead of scrolling. These aren't just good habits

—they're *votes* for your future. Each time you delay gratification, you cast a vote for the kind of life you want to live—not just the one you want to feel today.

And over time, those votes accumulate. You don't just build a bank account—you build *character*. You don't just grow money—you grow *mastery*. And perhaps most importantly, you grow *trust in yourself*. Because every time you keep a promise to your future, you reinforce the belief that you are capable of self-governance. That you are not a puppet of your emotions or a victim of your environment—you are an agent of choice.

This self-trust is the true wealth behind financial wealth. It's what allows you to stick with a plan during downturns, resist temptation during booms, and walk your own path when others chase trends. It's the quiet confidence that says, "I don't need to have everything now. I'm building something bigger."

And make no mistake—delayed gratification doesn't mean *denial*. It doesn't mean living a joyless life, depriving yourself of everything until some far-off date. That's a recipe for resentment, not success. The key is balance: enjoying today in a way that doesn't compromise tomorrow. Savoring the present without sabotaging the future.

That balance is different for everyone. For some, it's about budgeting luxuries. For others, it's about automating savings so they can spend freely with the rest. For many, it's about redefining what *enough* means, so they stop chasing things that don't actually fulfill them.

Because here's another truth: much of what we buy is not for joy—but for relief. Relief from stress. From boredom. From comparison. We scroll and spend not because we're deeply excited, but because we're temporarily *numb*. Delayed gratification interrupts this cycle. It forces us to confront the *real* emotion underneath the impulse—and often, that emotion has nothing to do with the item we're about to buy.

This is where financial health and emotional health intersect. The more we understand our motivations, the less we fall prey to them. The more we question our urges, the more freedom we create. Not the freedom to *do* whatever we want—but the deeper freedom to *choose* what truly matters.

Let's bring this back to wealth.

Most people are not broke because they're underpaid. They're broke because they spend without thinking. They mistake lifestyle for happiness. They chase status instead of security. And the one thing that could change everything—the ability to wait, to pause, to plan—is dismissed as boring, unrealistic, or too slow.

But the people who master money are almost always the ones who master *themselves* first. They don't need to time the market because they're already winning the *inner* game. They don't need to make millions because they know how to manage thousands. They aren't immune to temptation—but they've built systems, habits, and environments that support better choices.

And that's what delayed gratification is really about: creating a life where good decisions are easier, not harder.

Want to strengthen your delayed gratification muscle? Start here:

- **Automate your good behavior.** Set up automatic transfers to savings or investments. Remove willpower from the equation.

- **Track your wins.** Keep a journal of the times you waited, resisted, or chose long-term. Watch your confidence grow.

- **Visualize the reward.** Picture your future self. Where do they live? How do they feel? What did they need you to do today?

- **Replace, don't just remove.** If you cut out impulse spending, replace it with something meaningful: a walk, a book, a call with a friend.

- **Celebrate restraint.** When you *don't* buy something, congratulate yourself. You just invested in your future freedom.

Above all, remember this:

In a world that glorifies instant gratification, your ability to wait becomes a competitive advantage. While others trade freedom for pleasure, you are building something real. Something enduring. Something that, when it finally arrives, will feel not just satisfying—but *earned*.

Delayed gratification may not be flashy. It may not earn applause. But it will quietly make you powerful. And in a society addicted to speed, that kind of power is revolutionary.

Because the person who can wait is the person who can *win*.

The Psychology of Long-Term Thinking

If there's one concept that quietly separates those who struggle financially from those who thrive, it isn't intelligence, education, or even opportunity—it's *time perspective*. More specifically, it's the ability to think long-term. The capacity to zoom out far enough from the noise of the present moment and make decisions based not on today's urgency, but on tomorrow's possibilities. And though it may sound simple, this skill—this psychological strength—is one of the rarest and most powerful financial tools in existence.

Because long-term thinking doesn't come naturally to us. As human beings, we're wired for immediacy. Our ancestors weren't planning retirement—they were surviving the next storm, the next hunt, the next winter. Their brains evolved to prioritize short-term rewards over long-term gains, because those rewards kept them alive. That hardwiring still lives in us, whispering in our ear every time we consider saving instead of spending, or waiting instead of reacting.

But in a modern world—where survival is no longer the primary concern and the biggest threats are often *self-inflicted*—this ancient wiring can become our downfall. The impulse to act quickly, to seek pleasure now, to respond emotionally to short-term setbacks—these instincts that once served us now sabotage us. Especially in money.

Long-term thinking is the antidote.

But make no mistake—it's a mindset, not a moment. It's not just about choosing the better outcome; it's about *training your mind* to value what can't be seen yet. It requires imagination, discipline, and the ability to live in two timelines at once: the present you're in, and the future you're building.

Let's unpack this, because the implications are enormous.

When you think long-term, you make *different decisions*. You save when others spend. You invest when others panic. You delay gratification, not because you like suffering, but because you see what others can't: the compounding impact of small actions repeated over decades. You realize that most of what feels urgent today won't matter tomorrow—but what feels insignificant today might matter *immensely* in twenty years.

Think of long-term thinking like planting a tree. No one claps when you bury the seed. No one cheers when you water it. And for the first few years, it barely grows. You might even forget it's there. But one day

—if you've been consistent, if you've protected it—it becomes a towering source of shade, strength, and security. Most people never get that far. They dig up the seed to check its progress. They abandon the plot for something that promises quicker results. They forget that *time* is not the enemy—it's the engine.

And this is where the psychology gets real.

Because long-term thinking isn't just about the future—it's about how you feel in the *present*. It's hard to wait. Hard to trust. Hard to stay disciplined when the payoff is invisible. When the market dips. When your savings feel stagnant. When others flash their new car, or their sudden success, or their risky win.

In those moments, your brain screams: "Do something! Move! Change strategy! Spend a little—what's the harm?" And if you don't have the emotional resilience to stay rooted in your long-term vision, you'll get swept up in short-term storms.

This is why long-term thinking is not a financial strategy. It's a *mental practice*. It's about developing the ability to pause before reacting. To separate signal from noise. To tolerate discomfort for the sake of deeper alignment.

It requires you to stop comparing your timeline to others'. Their highlight reel is not your benchmark. Their shortcuts are not your path. Their urgency is not your emergency. Long-term thinkers play a *different game*—one where consistency trumps brilliance, and patience outperforms talent.

But let's be honest: it's not sexy. There's no adrenaline rush in saying, "I'll just keep doing the smart, quiet thing for the next thirty years." There's no social media post that goes viral for staying the course. That's why so few people do it. Because it doesn't feel heroic—it feels ordinary. But here's the secret: the people with extraordinary results are almost always those who embraced ordinary actions, long enough for them to matter.

And this mindset doesn't just apply to investing. It shapes *everything*. Want to build wealth? Think long-term.

Want to build a business? Think long-term.

Want to master a skill, improve your health, deepen a relationship, or leave a legacy? It all requires the same thing: the willingness to *endure the present without proof*—because you believe in what you're building.

It's worth noting, too, that long-term thinking is not passive. It's not about waiting quietly for things to happen. It's about making intentional choices *now* that align with your future goals. It's about seeing time as your teammate—not a ticking clock, but a patient partner who rewards alignment, not urgency.

And sometimes, long-term thinking means saying no to short-term profit. No to the shiny opportunity. No to the thing that feels good but costs too much in focus, energy, or integrity. Because you've learned that *not all growth is worth it*. That some wins are actually distractions. That not everything that glitters will last.

So how do you train yourself to think long-term in a world that screams for now?

Start with your environment. Surround yourself with people who value vision. Who aren't swayed by the noise. Who understand that a quiet decade can lead to a powerful future. If everyone around you is rushing, you'll feel behind. If they're building slowly and intentionally, you'll feel permission to do the same.

Then look at your inputs. What are you consuming? Are you flooded with news, drama, and urgency? Or are you feeding your mind with ideas, principles, and strategies that stretch your timeline? The stories you hear daily shape the story you live.

Build systems that remove temptation. Automate your savings. Set rules for investing. Create friction for impulsive spending. The more you rely on willpower, the more vulnerable you are. Let your environment do the heavy lifting.

And most importantly, get clear on your *why*. The longer the game, the stronger the reason must be. What are you really building? Who are you building it for? What future version of yourself are you honoring with today's decision?

When your why is powerful, your patience becomes possible.

In the end, long-term thinking is an act of *love*. Love for your future self. Love for your family. Love for the life you're quietly designing. It's a declaration that you are more than your impulses. That you are capable of holding a vision across decades. That you are not chasing moments—you're building meaning.

And perhaps that's what makes it so powerful.

Because while others are busy reacting, you are *creating*. While they seek excitement, you seek endurance.

While they sprint, you walk.

And in walking, you arrive somewhere they never will—not because you were faster, or smarter, or luckier. But because you knew the secret.

That time is not something to fight or fear. It's something to *work with*.

And when you do, it becomes not a burden—

—but a blessing.

Chapter 7: Risk is Relative

Risk, in the abstract, feels like math. It looks like percentages on a spreadsheet or volatility charts in an investment portfolio. It appears to be something objective, something fixed and universally understood— like gravity or temperature. And yet, the moment we step outside the world of numbers and formulas and into the landscape of real human behavior, risk reveals itself to be something entirely different: not a number, but a feeling. Not a statistic, but a story. Not universal, but *personal.*

Risk is relative.

What feels risky to one person might feel perfectly safe to another. And not because one of them is irrational or reckless or naive—but because risk, as experienced by human beings, is filtered through a deeply subjective lens: shaped by past experiences, current emotions, future expectations, and even inherited beliefs passed down through families and cultures.

This relativity of risk is not just an interesting psychological observation—it's a foundational truth that explains why so many people make dramatically different financial decisions, even when facing the same information. It's why two investors can look at the same opportunity and one sees a threat, while the other sees freedom. It's why someone may avoid the stock market entirely while another invests aggressively. It's why real estate can feel like a goldmine to one person and a house of cards to another. The facts may be the same. The risks may be objectively identical. But the *felt* experience? Entirely different.

And here's the real problem: we rarely question our risk lens. Most of us assume that the way we perceive risk is how risk actually is. We believe that our comfort zones are accurate maps of danger and safety. And so, when we watch others make choices that don't match our comfort zone, we assume they're either foolish or fearless. But in reality, they're just seeing a different version of risk—one that's valid for *them*, even if it's invisible to us.

This is why so much personal finance advice fails. Because it assumes that risk tolerance is something static, measurable, and transferable. That if you just answer a few questions or take a quiz, your risk profile can be revealed and your financial decisions optimized. But in practice, risk is far messier. It fluctuates with your mood. It changes with your circumstances. It evolves with age, with experience, with wins and losses. It's as fluid as your sense of self—and that's what makes it so powerful, and so dangerous.

To understand this, we must explore the emotional roots of risk.

For some, risk is synonymous with loss. It's the memory of watching a parent lose a job or a home. It's the trauma of growing up in scarcity, where every dollar counted and every mistake had consequences. For others, risk is tied to identity. Taking a big swing—and missing—feels like failure not just of the plan, but of the *person*. Their self-worth is entangled with the outcome. Still others associate risk with freedom. The chance to break free from constraints, to bet on themselves, to escape the predictable. To them, not taking the risk feels like a prison.

And none of these stories are wrong. They're just incomplete.

Because the truth is, every financial decision involves risk. Playing it safe is risky. Saving too much is risky. Waiting too long is risky. Investing is risky. Not investing is risky. The question is never *if* risk exists—it's only *where*, and *how much*, and whether you can stomach the form it takes.

That's why copying someone else's financial strategy is often a mistake. Because unless you share their history, values, fears, and future plans, their risk tolerance isn't yours. What worked for them might break you. What terrifies them might energize you. There is no one-size-fits-all path because there is no one-size- fits-all definition of danger.

This is especially true in investing.

A 25-year-old entrepreneur with no dependents and high risk tolerance might throw 80% of their money into a high-growth index fund and sleep like a baby. A 60-year-old nearing retirement, having grown up during a financial crisis, might panic over a 10% dip and withdraw everything. Are either of them wrong? No. They're just playing different games. Living in different stories. Feeling different risks.

And yet, we judge. We mock those who play too safe. We envy those who gamble big and win. We shame those who panic-sell. But behind every decision is a brain trying to protect itself. A heart trying not to break again. A soul trying to find peace, not just profit.

So how do we navigate this deeply personal, often invisible landscape? It starts with self-awareness.

You must learn to recognize your own risk fingerprint. To trace the origins of your fear—or your boldness. Ask yourself: When do I feel most anxious about money? What memories shape that anxiety? What outcomes do I fear the most—not just financially, but emotionally? When have I taken a risk that felt right? When have I regretted not taking one?

These aren't easy questions. They require honesty. Sometimes even therapy. But they are necessary if you want to build a financial life that fits *you*, rather than one that merely looks good on paper.

Next, you must stop outsourcing your risk compass.

Financial media is filled with hot takes, urgent predictions, and confident voices telling you what to do. But they are not you. They don't live your life. They won't carry your consequences. Their advice may be well-intentioned—but if it clashes with your risk reality, it won't work. At best, it'll be ignored. At worst, it'll lead to decisions that feel smart in theory and unbearable in practice.

This doesn't mean you ignore advice. It means you *filter* it through your lived experience. It means you adapt principles to fit your priorities. It means you take what serves you and leave the rest.

And finally, you must accept that risk tolerance is not a destination—it's a conversation. Something you return to often. Something you revisit after each new season of life. What felt safe at 30 might feel reckless at 50. What felt terrifying after your first market crash might feel routine after the second. This flexibility isn't weakness—it's wisdom. Because the most powerful financial plan is not the one that's technically perfect. It's the one you can *stick with*.

The best investors are not the ones with the highest IQ. They're the ones with the strongest emotional endurance. The ones who understand that risk is less about numbers and more about nerves. Less about maximizing returns and more about minimizing regret.

And that's the heart of this chapter:

Risk isn't what the market does. It's what *you* feel when it happens. So stop asking, "Is this risky?"

Start asking, "Can *I* live with this risk?"

Because once you understand that risk is relative, you stop chasing perfect strategies. And start building a plan that fits something far more important—

Your *reality*.

What Feels Risky Isn't Always Risky

We live in a world governed not by pure logic, but by emotion, perception, and instinct. Nowhere is this more obvious than in the way we perceive risk. While textbooks and financial analysts would like to define risk as volatility, standard deviation, or drawdown percentages—terms that fit nicely into a spreadsheet and sound comfortably objective—what risk actually *feels* like to a human being navigating their financial life is something far more elusive, deeply subjective, and emotionally charged.

Because what feels risky isn't always what *is* risky—and that gap between perception and reality is where most financial missteps, regrets, and missed opportunities are born.

At its core, risk is meant to signal danger. It's our internal radar system, evolved to keep us alive. For our ancestors, that system was essential. If the bush rustled, it might be the wind—or it might be a predator. The people who assumed the worst tended to survive. In today's world, however, the rustling isn't coming from the underbrush—it's coming from the stock market, the real estate sector, the crypto graphs on our phones. Our ancient wiring still fires the same way, even when the threat is no longer immediate physical harm but a temporary dip in a retirement account or a missed career opportunity. And so, we flinch. We freeze. Or worse—we flee.

This emotional response to risk is so potent because it masquerades as logic. We feel something and mistake it for reason. We say, "This investment feels risky," or "That career move doesn't feel safe," and we accept the feeling as fact. We rarely stop to question: *Is it really risky? Or does it just feel unfamiliar? Uncomfortable? Out of sync with my past experiences?*

You see, the human brain struggles to distinguish between risk and uncertainty. Risk is measurable— there's data, probabilities, and historical context. Uncertainty, on the other hand, is what our brains hate most: the *unknown*. And so, we conflate the two. Anything unfamiliar, anything not guaranteed, anything that requires trust in the future—gets stamped with a warning label: **RISKY**. Even if, objectively, it's safer than what we're already doing.

Let's make that real.

To someone raised in a household where money was scarce and unpredictability was dangerous, the idea of investing in the stock market—even in a broad, low-fee index fund—can feel like gambling. They've been trained to believe that money should be held tightly, that safety is in cash, and that markets are a mysterious machine controlled by people who don't have their best interests at heart. To them, even a moderate investment might feel like a reckless risk.

Now imagine someone who grew up in a financially stable household where investing was normal, where recessions came and went without panic, and where long-term thinking was modeled. To this person, putting money in a diversified portfolio doesn't feel risky—it feels *responsible*. They might see *not* investing as the true danger.

Same investment. Same data. Two completely different emotional realities.

That's the paradox: the very same action can feel wildly risky to one person and completely safe to another—not because of facts, but because of *history*. Risk, as it turns out, is rarely about the thing itself. It's about the story we tell ourselves about what could happen, and whether we believe we could survive it.

And here's where it gets even more complex.

What feels *safe* can sometimes be the riskiest thing of all.

Take cash, for example. For many, cash feels like the ultimate safety net. You can see it, touch it, control it. It doesn't fluctuate. It doesn't disappear overnight. But in a world where inflation quietly erodes purchasing power year after year, holding too much cash over a long period is like standing on a slowly melting iceberg—you don't feel the danger until you're soaked.

Or consider staying in a job that drains your energy and erodes your confidence because it offers a "stable" paycheck. It feels safe in the short term. But what about the long-term cost? The opportunity cost of not growing? The emotional toll of chronic dissatisfaction? The risk of staying small when you were meant to grow?

We are incredibly good at rationalizing familiar discomfort as safety, and incredibly bad at recognizing the slow burn of deferred dreams and unnoticed erosion.

Why does this happen?

Because humans are wired to overweight short-term emotions and undervalue long-term consequences. We trade tomorrow's well-being for today's comfort. We avoid the temporary anxiety of change at the expense of deeper, more meaningful security. And when we do this repeatedly, we end up building lives that *look* safe but are, in fact, incredibly fragile—susceptible to burnout, financial stagnation, and missed potential.

The antidote? Learning to separate what *feels* risky from what *is* risky.

This is not easy. It requires deep introspection and an honest inventory of your emotional wiring. It means looking at the fears that drive your financial choices and asking whether they are rooted in truth—or just in trauma, habit, or inherited beliefs.

It also means learning to listen to discomfort without being ruled by it. Discomfort is not always danger. Sometimes it's just the stretching sensation of growth. Sometimes it's your mind catching up with a new, better version of what's possible.

When something feels risky, ask yourself: *What exactly am I afraid of?* Is it the potential outcome—or the emotion I would feel if that outcome happened? Am I afraid of losing money—or of what it would mean about me if I did? Am I afraid of the market crashing—or of feeling like a fool?

Often, our fear isn't of the event—it's of the *shame* that might follow. And when you realize that, you begin to take back power. You stop making decisions from a place of ego preservation and start making them from a place of long-term alignment.

This doesn't mean you ignore fear. Quite the opposite. You *respect* it—but you don't give it the steering wheel. You use it as a signal, not a sentence. You investigate it. You put it in context. You ask: *Is this fear protecting me—or limiting me?*

And sometimes, the boldest financial decision is the one that feels calm. Not because it's guaranteed—but because you've done the work to understand your own psychology. You've trained yourself to tolerate discomfort in service of growth. You've built the internal capacity to sit with uncertainty without letting it distort your perception of risk.

The greatest investors, entrepreneurs, and financially secure individuals aren't the ones who feel no fear. They're the ones who've learned to *interpret* fear. To distinguish between real threats and imagined ones. Between calculated risks and emotional overreactions.

Because what feels risky isn't always risky. And what feels safe isn't always safe.

And the person who learns to tell the difference—not through theory, but through self-awareness, emotional regulation, and long-term thinking—is the one who can walk through uncertainty with quiet confidence.

In the end, risk is not a red light. It's a yellow one.

It's a prompt to slow down, to pay attention, to evaluate—but not to retreat.

Because if you spend your life avoiding what feels risky, you may avoid loss—but you will also avoid *life*. And there is no greater risk than that.

Personal History Shapes Risk Perception

Every decision we make with money—whether to save or spend, to invest or hold back, to leap into opportunity or retreat into safety—is not made in a vacuum of logic, but rather against the deeply colored backdrop of our personal history. Risk, in this sense, is not a fixed number but a feeling sculpted by memory, experience, and emotion, and the stories we carry from the past cast long shadows across the choices we face in the present. Though the financial world tends to treat people as rational agents governed by interest rates, compound growth curves, and the objective metrics of risk tolerance assessments, the truth is that every one of us comes into our relationship with money already shaped by something far more potent and far less visible: our past.

A person who watched their parents lose their home during a financial crisis does not perceive risk the same way as someone who grew up in an environment where money was abundant and security was assumed. The first may associate debt with collapse, volatility with trauma, and opportunity with danger

—while the second may view the same volatility as a playground of possibility and the same debt as a normal stepping stone to growth. These contrasting perceptions are not about intelligence or discipline— they are about emotional imprinting, and until they are brought into conscious awareness, they quietly but powerfully govern everything we do.

Consider the simple act of investing. Two people may be presented with the same opportunity: a long- term fund, historically stable, backed by solid performance and logical data. The first sees risk—a potential loss that could shake the foundation of their fragile sense of security. The second sees progress— a chance to build wealth over time. They're not reading different prospectuses. They're reading from different internal scripts. One may have grown up hearing constant anxiety about bills, watching arguments break out over small purchases, learning to equate financial risk with emotional chaos. The other may have absorbed lessons about patience, compound interest, and the safety net of second chances. The same investment speaks in very different tones to each.

It's not just the events of the past that matter, but the *emotional conclusions* we drew from them. A child whose family lost everything may grow up either terrified of financial risk—or determined to never be in that position again, becoming bold and aggressive in their investing. Another child, growing up with wealth but emotionally neglected, may use money as a means to control relationships, mistaking accumulation for love or power. These reactions don't come from data—they come from pain, pride, fear, longing, and the unique texture of the lives we've lived.

Even subtle moments can have a deep impact. Think of someone who was scolded for spending too much on something they loved—a book, a piece of clothing, an experience. That shame doesn't vanish. It becomes internalized, possibly leading to a lifelong hesitation around spending on themselves, even when they can afford it. Or someone who witnessed a parent take a business risk that didn't pan out—maybe they went bankrupt, maybe they had to start over. That memory may become a cautionary tale, not just about entrepreneurship, but about trusting one's own ambition. They might grow up believing that boldness always ends in failure, not because it's true, but because that's the lesson the moment taught them.

And so we grow up building financial lives that look safe from the outside but are often constructed as a defense against ghosts from the past. We avoid investments not because they don't make sense, but because they awaken fears we haven't addressed. We hoard money because we're afraid to be vulnerable. We chase wealth because we think it will finally prove our worth. We work ourselves into the ground because once, long ago, someone told us we weren't enough unless we earned our place.

Until we examine the roots of these beliefs, they guide us like invisible hands.

What complicates this further is that we live in a culture that prizes external validation and often shames emotional honesty. Financial discussions are typically presented as neutral, data-driven conversations, where talking about the emotional side of money feels out of place or even weak. But ignoring emotion doesn't make it go away—it just drives it underground, where it does far more damage. The more we pretend our past doesn't influence our present, the more likely it is that we'll keep reliving it.

And here's the uncomfortable truth: your personal history isn't your fault, but it *is* your responsibility. You may not have chosen the financial lessons you learned as a child, the economic instability you endured, or the traumas that shaped your view of money—but if you want to have a healthy, sustainable relationship with risk, you must choose to become aware of them. Otherwise, you'll continue to make decisions not from clarity, but from reaction—from the unresolved fears of your past masquerading as present-day wisdom.

This requires reflection, and sometimes discomfort. You must be willing to ask hard questions: What early experiences shaped how I feel about risk? What stories did I absorb about wealth, poverty, ambition, and safety? How have those stories served me—and how have they limited me? What emotional rewards do I associate with financial success? What punishments do I fear if I fail? These are not questions with easy answers, but they are the doorway to freedom.

When you begin to separate your history from your present, you give yourself room to choose more deliberately. You may still feel fear when facing a financial risk—but now you understand *where* that fear comes from. You may still feel hesitation around investing—but now you can differentiate between actual danger and the echo of an old belief. You may still want to avoid debt—but now you can analyze whether it's the debt itself or the shame attached to it that drives your avoidance.

One of the greatest gifts you can give yourself is the clarity to say: "This fear is real—but it's not necessarily true." That single sentence opens up a new frontier. It allows you to honor your past without being imprisoned by it. It gives you the power to write a new financial narrative—not one dictated by inherited fears, but one aligned with your current reality and future goals.

It also cultivates compassion. When you understand that everyone is navigating risk through the lens of their own history, you stop judging others so harshly. You no longer see someone's reluctance as weakness or their boldness as recklessness—you see it as the expression of their unique emotional blueprint. And that empathy, extended toward others and yourself, creates the conditions for smarter, kinder, and more sustainable decisions.

Because risk isn't just about market performance or business models—it's about emotional safety, personal meaning, and lived experience. And your tolerance for it will never be found in a formula—it will be found in the way you relate to your own past.

Personal history doesn't just influence how we think about risk—it *defines* it. Until we realize that, we remain at the mercy of old scripts. But once we do, we gain something far more powerful than certainty.

We gain *agency*—the ability to choose not just what we do with our money, but who we become in the process.

The Danger of Copying Others' Strategies

In the era of viral success stories, bite-sized advice from financial influencers, and curated lifestyles presented as templates for achievement, it has become alarmingly easy to fall into the illusion that the right money strategy is simply a matter of imitation. We scroll through Instagram posts celebrating early retirement, binge-watch YouTube videos on stock-picking secrets, and consume podcasts that promise to decode the formula behind building wealth — all while quietly taking mental notes and adjusting our sails toward someone else's North Star. But beneath this flood of content and the appearance of wisdom lies one of the most overlooked yet dangerous tendencies in modern finance: copying someone else's strategy without first understanding your own reality.

The truth, as unglamorous as it may sound, is that personal finance is exactly that — *personal*. What works brilliantly for one person may fail catastrophically for another, not because one strategy is superior or inferior in isolation, but because each strategy is deeply entwined with the life, values, psychology, obligations, goals, and risk tolerance of the person implementing it. To assume that a method can be copied wholesale, stripped from its original context and applied to your own life with the same results, is to misunderstand how financial behavior really works.

Consider the example of aggressive investing. You might come across a twenty-eight-year-old entrepreneur who pours 90% of their net worth into growth stocks, cryptocurrencies, or startup ventures. They speak with conviction. They post screenshots of gains. They make it look exciting, even effortless.

And they tell you, with bold certainty, that *you should be doing the same.* But what they may not mention is that they live rent-free in their parents' home, have no dependents, no debt, and a high tolerance for volatility. Their baseline is padded with layers of psychological and practical safety nets. You, on the other hand, might be supporting a family, paying off student loans, and trying to build stability for the first time in your life. Applying their strategy to your situation isn't brave — it's reckless.

This is not just a matter of different lifestyles, but of different *foundations*. Every person brings to the table a unique combination of past experiences, future responsibilities, emotional triggers, and internal narratives. One person may thrive on high-risk, high-reward ventures because they associate risk with freedom and adventure. Another may avoid even modest financial risks because their earliest memories involve the trauma of scarcity and loss. Neither is right or wrong — but both are *true* for the person living them. And when we ignore these personal dimensions in favor of mimicking others, we don't just risk making poor financial decisions. We risk betraying ourselves.

The danger isn't only in the strategy itself, but in the psychological mismatch it creates. Let's say you force yourself to adopt a minimalism-inspired extreme saving approach — living on rice and beans, tracking every penny, cutting every joy-based expense — because someone online told you that's the path to early retirement. But what if you value experience, spontaneity, or generosity? What if living that way doesn't just create discipline but breeds quiet resentment, a sense of deprivation, or a loss of identity? You might stick with it for months or even years, but the internal cost accumulates like silent debt, and one day, you snap — abandoning the whole plan, sabotaging your progress, or worse, developing a toxic relationship with money altogether.

Or consider the inverse: you adopt a high-spending, "abundance mindset" financial approach, believing that thinking rich will make you rich. You invest in luxury experiences, expensive courses, and designer brands — because someone you follow claimed that visualizing wealth requires *embodying* wealth. But beneath the surface, you're drowning in credit card debt, lying awake at night, wondering how you'll cover next month's rent. The mindset isn't wrong — but the mismatch between your *financial reality* and the *image* you're trying to uphold becomes a source of deep cognitive dissonance and anxiety.

Copying someone else's strategy becomes even more dangerous when it's rooted in *their* strengths, not yours. A person who has a natural affinity for spreadsheets, data analysis, and discipline might thrive with a complex investing strategy involving real-time rebalancing, tax-loss harvesting, or advanced options trading. You, however, might be more intuitive, creative, and emotionally driven. Trying to mirror their system might not only exhaust you, but cause you to disengage entirely — not because you're lazy or incapable, but because it simply doesn't fit the way your brain is wired. The very tools that help one person succeed can become chains for someone else.

And yet, the pressure to imitate is everywhere. Social media algorithms reward bold claims, flashy success, and simplified narratives. Financial influencers are incentivized to present their story as a universal blueprint — not because they're malicious, but because relatability drives engagement, and engagement drives monetization. It's seductive to believe that if we just *do what they did*, we'll get what they have. But behind every post is a story we don't fully see: the unshared losses, the invisible privileges, the personal context that made their decisions reasonable *for them*.

There's also the ego trap. When we adopt someone else's strategy and it doesn't work for us, we don't usually blame the strategy. We blame *ourselves*. We assume we failed because we're not disciplined enough, not smart enough, not motivated enough. We internalize the failure as a reflection of our inadequacy, when in truth, the mistake was not in the execution — but in the assumption that someone else's path could be walked in our shoes.

The antidote to this isn't isolation or cynicism. It's discernment. It's learning to gather insights from others without surrendering your autonomy. It's asking not just *What are they doing?* but *Why are they doing it? What circumstances allowed that to work for them? Do I share those conditions? Do I share those values?*

Before you adopt a financial strategy, ask yourself:

- Does this align with my lifestyle, responsibilities, and emotional needs?
- Is this sustainable for me, or am I forcing myself to fit a mold?

- Am I doing this because it makes sense — or because I want to replicate someone else's results?

- Will this strategy still make sense *if no one sees it*? If I never post about it? If I don't get external validation?

Because the truest financial strategy — the one that will endure volatility, stress, and the changing seasons of your life — is not the one that sounds best on a podcast or looks best in a TikTok clip. It's the one that reflects your values, supports your goals, and respects your limits.

This doesn't mean you stop learning from others. In fact, one of the most powerful things you can do is study a wide range of financial approaches, not to find the *right* one, but to extract the principles that resonate, the lessons that translate, and the inspiration that encourages you to build your *own* system. Let their stories be reference points — not commandments. Let their success be motivation — not measurement.

There's no shame in taking time to experiment, to adapt, to change course when a strategy doesn't feel right. You are not failing when you adjust. You are calibrating. You are learning to listen not just to numbers but to *yourself*. Because at the end of the day, financial success isn't about getting rich quickly, or following the perfect plan, or outperforming others — it's about building a life that feels stable, meaningful, and true to you.

The danger of copying someone else's strategy isn't just that it might not work. It's that in trying to become them, you lose yourself.

And in finance — as in life — no return is worth that cost.

Building Your Own Financial Tolerance Scale

In the vast and noisy landscape of personal finance advice, one truth consistently gets overlooked: your ability to tolerate risk is not defined by your income, your job title, or how much financial content you've consumed — it's defined by how well you know yourself. And that kind of knowledge isn't built on spreadsheets or simulations, but through quiet observation, honest reflection, and a willingness to sit with your own fears, impulses, and values long enough to understand what truly drives you. Building your own financial tolerance scale is less about mastering the market and more about mastering your reactions to it

— knowing not just what you can afford to lose, but what you can emotionally withstand without compromising your peace, your judgment, or your values.

At its core, a financial tolerance scale is an internal compass. It's not a fixed formula or a personality quiz result. It's a dynamic understanding of what types of financial risk feel manageable, what causes panic, and where your unique edge lies — that subtle space between too much caution and too much recklessness. It's recognizing that while some people can sleep soundly through a 30% market drop, others might lie awake at night after reading one pessimistic headline. And both responses are valid — so long as they're understood and accounted for when making decisions.

The problem is, most people don't take the time to build this scale deliberately. Instead, they inherit a default setting from their upbringing, their peers, or their favorite financial influencer. They adopt investment strategies, spending habits, or savings goals that sound smart in theory but don't align with their lived emotional reality. And when those strategies backfire — when anxiety builds, or decisions become erratic, or results don't match expectations — they assume *they* are the problem, instead of realizing the strategy was simply misaligned with their own tolerance bandwidth.

The work begins by acknowledging that your risk tolerance is not a number — it's a spectrum shaped by multiple overlapping factors: emotional stability, financial security, past experiences, personality traits, goals, values, and even physical health. Someone with a high net worth but deep anxiety may have a lower effective risk tolerance than someone with modest means and a calm temperament. Someone who grew up with financial instability may crave predictability and avoid risk not because they lack intelligence, but because their nervous system equates volatility with danger. And someone who thrives on challenge and novelty might take risks that seem bold to others but feel energizing to them.

The first step in building your own scale is reflection — honest, unfiltered, sometimes uncomfortable reflection. Start with your past. Look at the financial decisions you've made over the last five to ten years. When did you feel calm and confident? When did you panic? What choices gave you peace, and which ones kept you up at night? What patterns can you observe? Was it timing the market that triggered stress, or was it overleveraging yourself? Was it investing in volatile assets, or ignoring your gut in favor of someone else's advice?

Write these down. Don't just generalize. Be specific. The more clearly you can see your past reactions, the more precisely you can design a future approach that honors your limits.

Next, assess your *current context*. Tolerance is not fixed — it shifts depending on your life stage, obligations, and emotional bandwidth. A young person with no dependents and a stable income may have the capacity to take greater risks than a new parent juggling debt, time pressure, and emotional exhaustion. Your job security, health, relationships, and even how well you've been sleeping can all influence your ability to handle financial uncertainty. A good financial plan is not one that looks perfect in theory — it's one that functions under the actual conditions of your life.

Then, consider your *values*. What are you really optimizing for? Is it freedom, stability, growth, legacy, contribution, peace of mind? Your tolerance scale should reflect not just what you can survive, but what supports the life you're trying to build. If peace is your top value, strategies that offer long-term rewards at the cost of constant stress may not be worth it. If growth is your primary driver, then some discomfort might be acceptable — even necessary — provided it's measured and meaningful.

This is also where *emotional honesty* becomes essential. Many people adopt high-risk strategies not because they align with their true goals, but because they want to appear bold, sophisticated, or financially savvy. Others avoid all risk not because it's wise, but because they fear failure, judgment, or shame. If your financial choices are being made to impress others or avoid criticism, you are not operating on your own scale — you are living inside someone else's.

The goal is to find your *edge* — that delicate space where you are challenged but not overwhelmed, stretched but not broken. Where the discomfort of growth exists, but does not drown out your sense of agency or clarity. And this edge isn't found once and forever — it must be revisited regularly, as your life changes, as your self-awareness deepens, and as your goals evolve.

To make this practical, try creating your own financial tolerance spectrum — a personal map of what kinds of decisions lie within your comfort zone, what lies just beyond it, and what triggers distress. For example:

- **Comfort zone:** Saving consistently, investing in index funds, tracking spending monthly.

- **Stretch zone:** Allocating a small portion to higher-risk assets, starting a side hustle, increasing investment contributions during market dips.

- **Distress zone:** Investing in things you don't understand, using leverage, following trends impulsively, letting emotions drive big decisions.

This spectrum is not static. It should grow with you. As your confidence, knowledge, and financial foundation deepen, you may find your stretch zone becoming your new comfort zone. The key is not to rush this evolution, but to let it unfold naturally, through experience and reflection — not pressure or comparison.

Also recognize that tolerance is not just about risk-taking, but about *persistence under pressure*. It's about how you behave when the inevitable uncertainty arrives — when the market crashes, when the business slows, when the plan goes off script. Your real tolerance is not how brave you feel when things are going well. It's how well you stick to your principles when they're being tested. And that kind of tolerance is built not through theory, but through small, repeated encounters with discomfort — decisions that stretch you just enough to grow your resilience without snapping your resolve.

Another often-missed dimension of tolerance is the *tolerance for waiting* — for long-term strategies that take time to bear fruit. Many people abandon sound plans not because they failed, but because they required patience. Building wealth, financial independence, or even simple peace around money is not a sprint — it's a slow layering of habits, decisions, and time. Your scale should include an honest look at how well you tolerate slow progress, and whether you're prone to abandoning good paths because the rewards aren't immediate.

Ultimately, building your own financial tolerance scale is about *agency*. It's about reclaiming your right to define success on your own terms, and to choose strategies that serve your actual life — not the life you think you should want. It's about exiting the comparison trap and committing to alignment. It's about knowing that wisdom doesn't mean taking no risk — it means taking the *right* risk for *you*.

When you build your financial plan from this place of internal clarity, something remarkable happens: your strategy may look boring to others, or unconventional, or slower — but it feels *right*. You sleep better. You make decisions more calmly. You stop second-guessing every move, because you're no longer borrowing convictions from others. You're living your own.

And in a world where so many are chasing someone else's definition of wealth, that kind of alignment is the rarest — and most valuable — asset of all.

Courage Isn't the Absence of Risk—It's Understanding It

Courage, as it's often misunderstood in the financial world, is seen through the lens of dramatic moves — quitting a job to start a business, betting big on an unknown stock, leveraging assets to pursue exponential growth. The myth says courage is boldness, the will to leap into the unknown without fear or hesitation, to charge ahead even when the path is unclear. But in truth, the deepest and most sustainable form of courage isn't found in defiance of risk — it's born from an intimate understanding of it. Real courage, in financial life and beyond, does not deny danger or discomfort. It acknowledges both, stares them down with clarity, and moves forward with full awareness of the consequences.

It is tempting, especially in a culture that glamorizes success stories and glorifies the bold, to believe that bravery is a kind of numbness — a lack of fear. But fear is not the enemy. Fear is information. It is your mind's way of protecting you from the unknown, from chaos, from loss. The key is not to eliminate fear, but to decode it — to understand what it's pointing to, whether it is warning you about something real or merely echoing an old narrative that no longer serves your present.

There is a vast difference between ignorance-fueled impulsiveness and wisdom-rooted bravery. The person who invests their entire savings into a speculative market trend without fully understanding the mechanisms, without a cushion or an exit plan, is not courageous — they're unprepared. The entrepreneur who starts a venture on a whim, having done no research and ignoring warning signs, is not fearless — they're blind to risk. What they mistake for bravery is often adrenaline — a powerful chemical response that mimics conviction, but lacks sustainability.

On the other hand, consider someone who has studied their field carefully, saved over time, tested small ideas on the side, and gradually built confidence in their ability to manage uncertainty. When they decide to take a leap — leaving a job, making an investment, starting something new — they're not doing it out of reckless abandon. They're doing it from a place of calm, informed readiness. They are still afraid, but they move anyway — not because they believe they can't fail, but because they've made peace with the fact that failure is survivable.

Understanding risk doesn't make it disappear. It reframes it. It strips it of distortion and hyperbole. It lets you see it not as a monster in the dark, but as a collection of potential outcomes, each with a probability and a cost. Courage is not about ignoring those costs — it's about accepting them, planning for them, and moving forward anyway.

This kind of courage requires introspection. It demands that you know what you're willing to lose, and what you're not. That you define, clearly, what success looks like *for you* — not for the market, not for your social circle, not for your parents or mentors or followers, but for the quiet part of you that actually lives with the consequences of your choices.

And this is where the real work begins — because many people don't know what they truly value. They think they want wealth, but they really want freedom. They think they're chasing returns, but they're trying to outrun shame. They think they fear losing money, but they actually fear judgment, or vulnerability, or the crumbling of an identity that's been built around appearing successful. Until you dig beneath the surface of your fears, your desires, and your relationship with uncertainty, you can't make courageous choices — only reactive ones.

Understanding risk also means understanding *yourself*. Some people are wired for volatility — they find excitement in uncertainty, they are energized by risk, and they recover quickly from setbacks. Others need stability, consistency, and the ability to plan. Neither is better — but confusing the two can be devastating. When you adopt someone else's level of risk tolerance as your own, you end up living with constant anxiety or numbing out completely. Courage is knowing where your line is — and choosing to walk to it, not past it.

It also means understanding *context*. A decision that looks risky on the surface may actually be conservative in disguise, if made in the right context. For example, a person quitting their job to start a business may seem brave — but if they've saved a year's worth of expenses, have a spouse with a stable income, and have already secured a few clients, the risk is far more calculated than it appears. Conversely, someone staying in a stable job for years, afraid to make a change, may seem responsible — but if that job is draining their health, stunting their growth, and providing no upward trajectory, the *real* risk may be in staying.

In this way, courage often looks like patience. It looks like declining a tempting offer because you know it doesn't align with your long-term vision. It looks like sitting in cash when everyone else is chasing returns, because you're not ready — and that's okay. It looks like asking hard questions, saying "I don't know," and refusing to be rushed by other people's timelines. It looks like walking away from a good deal because it would cost you your peace. It looks like admitting that you need more time, more clarity, more learning — not because you're weak, but because you're committed to making decisions with your whole self, not just your ego.

Courage, then, is quiet. It is not loud or performative. It doesn't need an audience. It doesn't always look impressive from the outside. Sometimes it looks like saying no. Sometimes it looks like staying put.

Sometimes it looks like changing your mind. And sometimes, it looks like starting again — after a failure, after a setback, after realizing that the path you were on was never really yours to begin with.

It's also deeply personal. What is courageous for one person may be easy for another. Your friend might be comfortable investing thousands into real estate — not because they're braver, but because they've done it before, or because they have support, or simply because their emotional blueprint is different. For you, making your first $500 investment might feel like climbing Everest. That doesn't mean you're behind. It means your courage looks different. And that's valid.

The financial world doesn't reward quiet courage. It rewards returns, drama, and the illusion of control. But your real reward — the one that lasts — is peace of mind, clarity of purpose, and the ability to move through life without betraying yourself in pursuit of someone else's idea of success. That kind of reward isn't always measurable — but it is always *felt*. It's in the steadiness you bring to difficult conversations.

The sleep you don't lose at night. The confidence with which you say "This is enough" — not because it's what others would settle for, but because you've defined your *own* version of enough.

So don't chase the absence of fear. Don't wait for perfect certainty. Don't think you have to be bold in the way others are bold. Instead, learn to sit with risk. Learn its language. Understand what it's trying to teach you — about the world, and about yourself.

Then make your move — not from fear, not from pressure, not from ego, but from understanding. That is what real financial courage looks like.

And it is more than enough.

Chapter 8: Habits Trump Knowledge

In a world where intelligence is often treated as the ultimate currency, where credentials are paraded as proof of future success and financial acumen is assumed to belong to those who can speak in fluent economic jargon, it is quietly — and crucially — true that knowledge alone is rarely what separates the wealthy from the struggling. The truth, stripped of pretense and theory, is far simpler and more grounded in reality: how you behave matters far more than how much you know. And the behaviors that move the needle over time — the ones that compound, endure, and protect — are not the flashes of brilliance or the bursts of discipline, but the steady, often boring habits that form the foundation of a financially healthy life.

We live in a culture obsessed with optimization. We want the perfect investment strategy, the most tax-efficient structure, the smartest hack for early retirement. We binge financial podcasts, read books on wealth accumulation, subscribe to newsletters promising the next big thing. And yet, for all this information, the results remain uneven. People who "know better" often still make poor choices. People who lack formal education sometimes build vast fortunes. Why? Because behavior — not intellect — is the true engine of financial success. And behavior is shaped not by what we understand in moments of clarity, but by what we repeat when no one is watching.

This is where habits enter the picture — quiet, unassuming, often underestimated, and yet more powerful than any financial theory you can name. Habits are the autopilot of your financial life. They are the invisible scripts you follow each day, the small decisions you make without much thought, the behaviors that compound whether or not you realize they're compounding. Whether it's saving a small percentage of your income every month, reviewing your spending weekly, avoiding lifestyle inflation, or simply choosing not to act on fear when markets dip — these tiny, repeated actions build a scaffolding around your money life. And over time, that scaffolding becomes a fortress.

It's tempting to believe that dramatic change comes from dramatic action. That we need to overhaul our entire financial system, launch a business overnight, or suddenly become frugal monks to transform our relationship with money. But real change — lasting, sustainable change — is born in the mundane. It's born in choosing, again and again, to follow through on the small, repeatable behaviors that reflect the person you want to become. A budget isn't powerful because it's complicated — it's powerful because it's followed. A savings account isn't impressive because it earns high interest — it's impressive because it's funded consistently, even when it's inconvenient.

What habits offer — that knowledge does not — is structure. Discipline. Stability. When you build habits around your money, you take your emotions out of the equation. You don't have to decide every day whether to save or spend. You don't have to debate with yourself about whether to invest. You simply follow the system you've already designed — and the consistency of that system protects you from the volatility of your moods, your environment, and the market itself.

Moreover, habits create identity. When you show up for yourself financially every day — even in small ways — you begin to believe something new about who you are. You are no longer someone who struggles with money. You are someone who saves. Someone who plans. Someone who invests, not just in stocks or funds, but in themselves. And that shift in identity — that sense of being a person who follows through — is more valuable than any financial tip you'll ever receive.

Of course, building habits requires patience. And patience is not sexy. It's not flashy. It doesn't win you applause. But patience is the price of lasting wealth. It's the mindset that says, "I don't need this today if it will cost me tomorrow." And habits, when built well, train patience into your bones. They teach you to think long-term not because you've memorized the theory of compound interest, but because you've lived it. Because you've seen what happens when consistent effort, no matter how small, is given time to grow.

This chapter is a reminder — and an invitation — to shift your focus from the overwhelming complexity of financial perfection to the manageable simplicity of daily action. It's an argument for structure over spontaneity, for systems over smarts, for routines over resolutions. Because in the end, the gap between people who do well with money and those who don't is rarely a gap in intelligence. It is a gap in behavior. And behavior is built, moment by moment, habit by habit.

In the following sections, we'll explore why systems matter more than raw intellect, how tiny financial routines silently shape your future, how automation can protect you from your worst impulses, why consistency will always outpace complexity, and how the daily choices you make — or fail to make — are constructing your financial character, brick by brick.

This is not a call to know more.

This is a call to *do better, more consistently* — and to trust that even the smallest good habit, faithfully practiced, is worth more than the flashiest strategy left undone.

Why Systems Matter More Than Smarts

We live in a culture that places intelligence on a pedestal. From a young age, we are conditioned to believe that being smart is the golden ticket to success, that the most intelligent person in the room will naturally rise to the top, and that complex problems demand equally complex solutions understood only by the few who can grasp them. This belief infiltrates every facet of life — especially when it comes to money. But here's the quiet truth that undermines the myth: it's not the smartest who thrive financially. It's those with the best systems. Intelligence without systems is like a powerful engine with no steering wheel — it might roar with potential, but it's directionless, erratic, and prone to crashing. A system, even a simple one, gives that power form. It transforms knowledge into action, and action into results.

Financial life isn't an IQ test — it's a behavior test. And behavior, unlike intelligence, is not spontaneous. It's structured. It's shaped, trained, and reinforced through systems. Systems are what allow you to show up for your goals on the days you don't feel like it, when the market is crashing, when fear whispers in your ear, or when life throws curveballs that disrupt your best intentions. A good system turns discipline into default. It takes the burden of decision-making off your already exhausted mental plate and replaces it with structure that does the heavy lifting for you.

Think about how most people approach money. They learn a piece of financial advice — maybe about investing in low-cost index funds or budgeting with the 50/30/20 rule — and they think, "That makes sense." But then comes the chaos of daily life. Work stress. Emotional spending triggers. Emergencies. Uncertainty. And that knowledge, so crisp and clear in a calm moment, is nowhere to be found when it's actually needed. Not because the person is stupid. Not because the advice was wrong. But because they didn't have a system to catch them when their willpower inevitably faltered. The best plan means nothing if it's not built into your life as a repeatable habit — and that's what systems are for.

Systems are boring by design. They remove drama. They replace adrenaline with predictability. They aren't designed to feel exciting or heroic. In fact, the best systems often feel underwhelming — like setting up automatic transfers from checking to savings, or deciding in advance how much to invest each month, or reviewing your finances at the same time every week. These don't sound like breakthroughs. But they are — because they remove friction. And when you remove friction, you remove excuses. You remove inconsistency. You remove emotional interference.

Let's take investing as a case study. Many people obsess over which stocks to pick, when to enter the market, what indicators to follow. They consume mountains of financial content, track economic trends, and follow expert commentary. And yet, they underperform not because they lack knowledge, but because they lack consistency. They try to time the market, react to news cycles, chase trends, and bail during downturns. Meanwhile, the person with a basic system — a monthly automatic contribution to a diversified index fund — ends up building wealth slowly, quietly, and with far less stress. Why? Because their system works even when their emotions don't.

This doesn't mean systems eliminate risk or guarantee perfection. It means they reduce reliance on your moment-to-moment judgment — which is often your worst enemy in financial matters. Your emotions, biases, stress levels, and even the quality of your sleep can sabotage good decisions. Systems bypass this volatility. They lock in good behavior, not as a series of conscious choices, but as defaults.

A system doesn't have to be complex. In fact, the simpler it is, the more likely it is to endure. A simple weekly routine of checking your spending and adjusting your budget can do more for your financial health than reading ten personal finance books. A one-page investment policy that outlines your asset allocation, risk tolerance, and what you will do during a market crash is more useful than hours spent on Reddit or CNBC. Because it gives you a map. And when panic clouds your judgment, a map is better than a memory.

But here's the thing most people overlook: building a system requires humility. It requires acknowledging that you, like every other human, are prone to error. That you won't always be in the right mindset. That you will get tired, emotional, distracted. Smart people often struggle with this, because they believe they can outthink chaos. They believe they will always make rational choices. But intelligence doesn't immunize you against emotion. And in fact, the smarter you are, the more convincing your rationalizations will be when you want to make a poor decision.

That's why systems matter more than smarts — because they don't rely on your brilliance. They rely on your willingness to be honest with yourself, to anticipate your own weaknesses, and to create a structure that protects you from them. A smart person with no system might build wealth fast — and lose it just as fast. A less knowledgeable person with a solid, boring, repeatable system might build slowly — and keep it for life.

Let's zoom out even further. Systems are not just about spreadsheets or automation. They're about rhythm. Ritual. Predictability. A system is anything that removes choice from the equation and replaces it with intention. It's choosing in advance how you'll act, so you don't have to decide in the moment. This applies to every domain of your financial life — how you spend, how you save, how you invest, how you track your progress.

Want to build savings? Create a system where your savings are transferred automatically before you even see the money. Want to reduce spending? Create a rule that limits impulse purchases by requiring a 24- hour waiting period. Want to invest consistently? Automate contributions to your portfolio and remove the app from your phone so you're not tempted to tinker. These are systems. And they work not because they're glamorous, but because they remove the need for willpower — a finite resource.

And here's something else: systems scale. Once you build a system that works for your current income, it can adapt to higher income. Once you develop a system for tracking net worth or managing debt, you can apply it to more complex scenarios later. Systems grow with you. They evolve. But they must begin — and that beginning often feels small. Insignificant. But like compound interest, the effect of a good system isn't obvious right away. It's cumulative. Quiet. But over time, it becomes undeniable.

In contrast, intelligence is less scalable in this context. Knowing more doesn't guarantee doing better. In fact, more knowledge without action can lead to paralysis. You know too many strategies, hear too many opinions, and end up doing nothing. Or worse, doing too much. Constant tweaking. Second-guessing.

Overanalyzing. Systems cut through that noise. They provide clarity. Boundaries. Direction.

In the end, the financially successful are not always the smartest — they are the most consistent. They are the ones who respect the power of systems, who trade short-term excitement for long-term reliability. Who understand that wealth is not the result of one brilliant decision, but of thousands of unremarkable ones executed faithfully.

So if you're wondering where to begin, don't ask, "What should I know?" Ask instead, "What can I *do* consistently?" Then build a system around it — one that works with your life, your goals, and your temperament. Let the system carry the weight. Let it hold your future steady, even when your present feels unsteady.

Because in the end, it's not your brilliance that will build your financial legacy. It's your systems.

Financial Routines That Build Wealth Silently

There's something profoundly unglamorous about the idea of a routine. It lacks spectacle. It doesn't spark envy. It won't get attention at parties or likes on social media. Routines aren't loud — they don't shout their value. They are quiet, predictable, and often dismissed as mundane. Yet, beneath their modest surface, routines carry extraordinary power — the kind that doesn't manifest in dramatic headlines or sudden windfalls, but in the quiet accumulation of financial resilience, security, and eventual abundance. In truth, most wealth is not built in public — it's built in the privacy of daily disciplines, in the silent rituals that no one sees, in the habits that run beneath the surface of life like a steady current carving out a new landscape.

If you were to peek behind the curtain of a financially stable life, you wouldn't find chaos, genius, or perpetual hustle. You'd find systems. But even more granular than systems, you'd find routines — small, repetitive behaviors that serve as the scaffolding for every sound financial outcome. These are not necessarily groundbreaking actions. They are not the kind of things that make you feel brilliant or brave. But they are the things you do consistently, and they matter more than almost anything else.

There's a cultural tendency to romanticize spontaneity and chase excitement. We're told to "think big," to pursue bold moves, to innovate our way to success. And while innovation has its place, it is a poor substitute for structure. Because without a structure to support it, even the most visionary idea will collapse under the weight of inconsistency. Financial routines, by contrast, are unyielding. They don't require inspiration. They don't bend to mood. They function whether or not you feel like it — and that is their strength.

What do these routines look like in practice? They can be as simple as checking your accounts once a week, reviewing your spending every Sunday evening, contributing a fixed percentage of your income to savings every time you get paid, or allocating time monthly to review and rebalance your portfolio. Each of these routines, taken in isolation, may seem insignificant. But over time, they become powerful. They provide awareness, direction, and most of all — consistency. And consistency is what turns ordinary behavior into extraordinary results.

Consider the person who reviews their spending weekly. They aren't doing anything revolutionary. But by building this routine, they create awareness around their habits. They begin to see patterns. They catch small leaks before they become floods. They course-correct in real time, not six months later when a problem has compounded. This awareness, maintained consistently, is a kind of financial hygiene. And like brushing your teeth, it doesn't require genius — only commitment.

Or take the simple act of saving a fixed amount from every paycheck. It might feel robotic. It might not always feel necessary. But over time, it builds. It becomes automatic. It becomes identity. It moves from action to reflex. And perhaps most importantly, it creates a psychological buffer — a sense of control, stability, and forward motion that helps you stay grounded during turbulent times. That kind of internal peace is hard to measure, but impossible to fake.

The beauty of routines is that they are self-sustaining. Once established, they require very little cognitive effort to maintain. In fact, the effort comes not from doing the routine — but from *not* doing it. Once a routine is anchored in your life, skipping it creates friction. You feel off-balance, like you've missed something. And that internal accountability becomes more effective than any external pressure. It is the quiet voice that says, "We do this — because this is who we are."

Routines also help you make better decisions under pressure. When you're facing a financial emergency, a market downturn, or an unexpected opportunity, your routines provide a baseline of normalcy. They give you something to return to — a structure to fall back on. Instead of reacting impulsively, you respond from a place of groundedness. You already have habits in place that protect you. You've been practicing discipline in small ways, and now it scales when you need it most.

But perhaps the most overlooked benefit of financial routines is that they create space — space in your mind, in your schedule, in your emotional bandwidth. When you have a routine, you don't have to *think* about your finances constantly. You don't have to worry about whether you've saved this month or if your spending is off track. You've already built in check-in points. You trust the process. And that trust creates calm. That calm becomes confidence. And that confidence, in turn, allows you to focus on what really matters — building a life, not just a balance sheet.

It's important to note that not all routines are helpful. Some are born from fear, avoidance, or control. Obsessively checking your portfolio multiple times a day isn't a routine — it's a compulsion. Reviewing your finances obsessively because you're afraid of missing something isn't healthy discipline — it's anxiety in disguise. The most effective routines are grounded in clarity, not fear. They are built around your goals, not your insecurities. They serve your values, not your ego.

So, how do you build a routine that works? Start small. One routine. One behavior. One moment in your week that you claim for your financial well-being. Make it sacred. Make it non-negotiable. Maybe it's ten minutes every Monday morning to update your spending. Maybe it's a monthly ritual with your partner to review shared goals. Maybe it's an automatic transfer that happens the moment your paycheck lands.

Whatever it is, keep it simple. Keep it sustainable. Make it so easy you can't not do it. Then, once it becomes second nature, add the next one.

Over time, you'll build a rhythm — a cadence — that begins to define not just how you handle money, but how you see yourself in relationship to it. You are no longer reacting. You are engaging. You are not guessing. You are monitoring. You are not hoping. You are acting. And this shift — from passive to active, from erratic to intentional — changes everything.

Wealth doesn't need to be loud. It doesn't need to be fast. It doesn't need to arrive with fireworks. In fact, the most sustainable wealth is often built in silence — in the invisible routines that no one claps for, no one comments on, no one even notices. But you notice. You feel the difference. You feel the steadiness. You feel the sense of control that grows not from knowing everything, but from doing *something* — consistently, quietly, and with purpose.

So don't underestimate the power of what seems ordinary. Don't wait for motivation. Don't chase perfection. Choose a routine. Build it. Honor it. Let it carry you.

Because in the end, wealth is not a moment. It's a rhythm. A quiet drumbeat in the background of your life, echoing with every intentional act.

And that rhythm is how you rise.

Automating Good Behavior

There is a quiet irony in the fact that most people assume personal finance is about control, when in reality, the people who do best with money are often the ones who give up control — or rather, who design systems that don't require them to constantly exert it. Because control, when it relies solely on willpower or real-time decision-making, is a fragile tool. It fails us in the heat of emotion, in the fog of stress, in the fatigue of ordinary life. It falters when we are tired, distracted, tempted, or afraid. And so, if you want your financial behaviors to be consistent — not just occasionally good, but reliably good — you have to remove the need for constant control. You have to remove the choice altogether. That's where automation enters the picture — not as a luxury or a convenience, but as a cornerstone of behavioral success.

Automation is not simply about saving time or streamlining tasks. It is, at its core, about eliminating the friction that sabotages good intentions. Because if you study the gap between what people say they want to do with money and what they actually do, you'll find that it's rarely a lack of knowledge that holds them back. Most people know they *should* save more, spend less, invest regularly, and avoid debt. The problem isn't the knowing — it's the doing. Or rather, the *remembering to do, choosing to do,* and *following through when the moment comes.* And that's where things fall apart. Emotions rise. Impulses override plans. And the path of least resistance — which rarely aligns with our long-term goals — wins again.

Automation short-circuits that entire process. It turns good intentions into default behavior. It takes willpower out of the equation and replaces it with pre-committed action. When you automate a behavior, you're not just simplifying a task — you're making a decision once, in a calm, rational state, and locking it in so that future-you — stressed, busy, tempted, or overwhelmed — doesn't have to negotiate with your goals again.

Take, for example, the act of saving money. Most people think of saving as an active choice — something they have to decide to do each month. But that approach leaves room for inconsistency. One month you're motivated, the next month you're not. One month you have a surplus, the next you overspend. And slowly, despite your best intentions, your saving rate drops. But if you automate the process — if you set up a transfer that moves money from your checking to your savings or investment account the moment your paycheck arrives — you remove the choice. Saving happens first, not last. It happens by default, not by effort. And over time, that single automation can transform your financial trajectory.

The same principle applies to investing. One of the most powerful habits in wealth-building is regular, consistent investing — regardless of market conditions. But it's also one of the hardest habits to maintain manually, because markets are noisy, emotions are volatile, and news cycles are designed to provoke panic or euphoria. If you try to invest manually every month, you'll likely hesitate when markets dip, or over- invest when they rise. You'll second-guess your timing. You'll get caught in analysis paralysis. But if you automate your investments — through a payroll deduction, a recurring transfer, or a retirement plan — you bypass all of that. You invest no matter what. And that consistency, over years and decades, matters far more than your timing ever could.

But automation isn't just for saving or investing. You can automate debt payments, bill payments, charitable giving, budget tracking, and even calendar reminders to review your financial goals. You can automate alerts that notify you when your balance dips too low, or when a bill is due, or when a spending category exceeds its limit. You can build a system of nudges and defaults that essentially turns your financial life into a well-oiled machine — not perfect, but predictably functional. And in a world full of uncertainty, predictable functionality is a superpower.

Of course, some people resist automation. They fear losing flexibility. They worry they won't be able to adapt if their situation changes. But the truth is, automation doesn't remove control — it enhances it. It gives you more bandwidth to think strategically instead of reactively. It frees your mind from the noise of micro-decisions and lets you focus on the big picture. You can always update your automations when your goals or circumstances change. But you don't have to wrestle with them daily. That's the difference between living in a reactive spiral and operating within a proactive structure.

Automation also helps with one of the most overlooked challenges in personal finance: decision fatigue. Every day, you make hundreds of small choices — what to eat, what to wear, when to exercise, how to reply to emails, what to prioritize at work, whether or not to check social media, and on and on. By the time you get to your finances, your decision-making power is already depleted. That's when you're most vulnerable to bad choices — overspending, ignoring your goals, procrastinating on tasks that feel complicated or uncomfortable. Automation removes that vulnerability. It says: "This decision has already been made." And in that moment, you are protected — not by effort, but by design.

There is also a psychological benefit to automation that often goes unspoken: the sense of progress. When you automate good behavior, you get to feel — on a deep, subconscious level — that you are moving forward, even when you're not actively engaged. Your money is working. Your habits are building. Your system is running. That sense of progress, even if invisible day-to-day, creates momentum. And momentum breeds confidence. Confidence, in turn, makes it easier to continue doing the right things — not because you're forcing yourself to, but because they've become a part of who you are.

In a way, automation turns behavior into identity. You are no longer someone who *tries* to save. You are someone who saves. You are no longer someone who *wants* to invest. You are someone who invests. And identity is sticky. Once you see yourself a certain way, you begin to protect that identity. You make choices that reinforce it. That's the real power of automated behavior — not just that it works mechanically, but that it reshapes how you see yourself in relation to your money.

Still, automation isn't a magic wand. It won't work if you haven't done the foundational thinking about what you *want* your money to do. You still need clarity. You still need intention. Automation is a tool —

not a substitute for vision. But once you have that vision, automation becomes the bridge that connects your present behavior to your future reality. It becomes the mechanism through which consistency is made effortless, and goals become not just possible, but probable.

There's also something deeply human about designing systems that compensate for our flaws rather than pretending they don't exist. Automation is, at its best, an act of self-compassion. It says: "I know I will be tired. I know I will be distracted. I know I will be tempted to spend impulsively, to avoid the uncomfortable tasks, to delay the important conversations. So instead of expecting myself to be superhuman, I will design a system that catches me when I fall." That kind of honest, empathetic self-awareness is more powerful than all the financial theories in the world.

In the final analysis, the most important financial behaviors are not the ones you perform with great effort or in moments of peak discipline. They are the ones that happen whether or not you feel like doing them. And the only way to guarantee that kind of consistency is through automation.

So if you're looking for a place to start — start small. Automate one thing. Automate a weekly savings transfer. Automate your bill payments. Automate a contribution to your retirement account. Then automate the review of those automations — quarterly, biannually, whatever works for you. Layer by layer, build a financial system that removes as many decisions as possible, so that your energy is reserved for what truly matters.

Because in the end, good behavior isn't about trying harder. It's about designing smarter.

And nothing designs your future with more grace, more efficiency, and more resilience than the quiet, consistent power of automation.

Consistency Over Complexity

There is a kind of intellectual seduction that accompanies the search for financial success — a whispering allure that tells us that the answer must be hidden somewhere deeper, buried within intricate strategies, sophisticated products, or abstract economic theories accessible only to those fluent in the language of finance. And yet, for all the algorithms, formulas, and complex investment models that populate the financial world, the truth remains staggeringly simple: consistency beats complexity. Over and over again. Not just in theory, but in the quiet reality of actual outcomes. Because wealth, in its most sustainable form, is not a reward for brilliance — it is a byproduct of doing the simple things, again and again, especially when it's boring, inconvenient, or emotionally uncomfortable.

The modern world doesn't make this truth easy to believe. We are inundated with noise. Every day, a new voice proclaims the discovery of a shortcut, a smarter hack, a revolutionary framework. Financial influencers churn out content designed to provoke FOMO and confusion in equal measure. Headlines scream about market movements, currency fluctuations, and economic forecasts. And in the midst of all this complexity, we lose sight of the fundamentals. We begin to feel as though we're not doing enough — or that doing "just the basics" is somehow naive or lazy. But the opposite is true. Simplicity, when applied consistently, is not a sign of ignorance. It is a sign of clarity, of restraint, of mastery.

Think of the most consistently wealthy individuals — not just in net worth, but in stability, peace of mind, and long-term financial growth. These are not always the hedge fund managers or the high-frequency traders. More often, they are the people who saved diligently, lived slightly below their means, avoided lifestyle inflation, stayed invested through bear and bull markets alike, and chose strategies they understood well enough to stick with during periods of uncertainty. They weren't chasing novelty — they were honoring discipline. And discipline, over long periods of time, does what genius cannot: it endures.

Let's imagine two investors. The first is intellectually gifted, spends countless hours researching the market, fine-tuning a portfolio, reading whitepapers, and shifting allocations in real time based on macroeconomic trends. The second picks a simple, diversified index fund and invests a fixed percentage of their income every month, automatically, without adjusting for market noise. Twenty years later, it is entirely possible

— even likely — that the second investor has outperformed the first. Not because they were smarter, or faster, or more informed — but because they were consistent. They didn't try to optimize every decision. They didn't overthink. They just stuck to the plan.

That's the insidious part of complexity: it gives us the illusion of control. It makes us feel productive. It flatters our ego. We believe that if we're doing something complicated, we must be doing something important. But complexity often masks fragility. The more moving parts a plan has, the more opportunities it has to break. The more nuanced your strategy, the more tempted you'll be to abandon it the moment the environment changes. And when it comes to your finances, what matters most is not what you do in the best of times, but what you *still do* in the worst of times.

Consistency is durable. It is quiet. It is not dramatic or impressive at a glance. But it builds momentum. Every small act — every automatic contribution, every avoided impulse purchase, every monthly budget review — compounds over time. And compounding, as every seasoned investor knows, is not just a financial principle. It is a behavioral one. Habits compound. Decisions compound. Integrity compounds. And so does inconsistency. A single lapse, in isolation, is harmless. But repeated lapses, driven by the chase for something newer, smarter, or more profitable, erode your foundation. Complexity makes those lapses more likely. Simplicity — sustained simplicity — reduces the surface area for failure.

It's worth noting, too, that consistency isn't about perfection. It's about reliability. You don't have to make the optimal decision every time. You just have to avoid the consistently *bad* decisions — overspending, panic-selling, ignoring your goals, chasing fads. And the best way to avoid those decisions is not to master every nuance of finance, but to make the good decisions so automatic that the bad ones never even tempt you.

This is especially important during times of uncertainty. When markets crash, when the economy falters, when personal circumstances change, complexity becomes your enemy. It paralyzes. It invites overreaction. It makes you doubt your framework. But consistency — especially consistency rooted in a simple plan — gives you something to anchor to. You don't have to know what will happen next. You just have to keep doing what you've always done. That steadiness, that refusal to panic, that willingness to stay the course — that is what separates those who preserve wealth from those who lose it in moments of emotional volatility.

Consider how this principle shows up in everyday life. Physical fitness is a domain riddled with complexity: new diets, cutting-edge workouts, revolutionary supplements. But we all know that the person who walks for thirty minutes every day, eats mostly whole foods, and sleeps well will outperform — in both health and longevity — the person who bounces from one extreme program to the next, despite their encyclopedic knowledge of nutritional science. The same holds true with money. You don't have to be a financial savant. You just have to be consistent. Simple behaviors, repeated endlessly, will eventually outpace sporadic brilliance.

Why, then, do we so often chase complexity? Part of it is cultural. We live in a world that rewards novelty. Simple is seen as insufficient. We conflate effort with value. If something doesn't feel hard, we assume it isn't worth doing. And we're constantly being marketed to — by products, by people, by platforms — that promise a smarter way. But smarter is not always better. In fact, the smartest move is often the one you can *actually sustain*. It's the strategy that works with your psychology, your habits, your lifestyle. Because what works on paper doesn't matter if it doesn't work in practice.

Another reason is ego. Complexity feels like sophistication. It allows us to signal intelligence. We can talk about advanced investing strategies at dinner parties. We can debate the implications of interest rate shifts. We can use language that makes us sound like insiders. But all the sophistication in the world doesn't matter if your behavior isn't aligned. And behavior is rarely improved by more information. It is improved by better systems, clearer boundaries, and simpler routines.

This isn't to say that complexity is always bad. In certain cases — for experienced investors, entrepreneurs, or those with unique financial goals — complexity can serve a purpose. But even then, it must be built on a foundation of simplicity. Because complexity without consistency is chaos. And the inverse — consistency within simplicity — is freedom.

It gives you mental freedom. You no longer waste energy on decisions that don't move the needle. You no longer suffer analysis paralysis. You no longer second-guess yourself every time the market twitches. You have a plan. You follow it. That's it. You sleep better. You think more clearly. And most importantly, you make space for the parts of life that actually matter — your relationships, your passions, your health — without letting money become a constant source of anxiety.

So how do you practice consistency over complexity in your own financial life?

You start by simplifying. Choose one savings goal. Automate it. Choose one investment strategy. Stick to it. Choose one system for tracking your spending. Don't switch apps every two weeks. Build a routine.

Protect it. Resist the urge to optimize constantly. You don't need to do more. You need to do less — but more faithfully.

Measure your progress not by how clever your plan is, but by how long you've stuck to it. Reward yourself not for intensity, but for duration. Celebrate the 12th month in a row you contributed to your IRA, not the one time you picked a winning stock. Value resilience over brilliance. Discipline over drama.

Sustainability over excitement.

Because in the final equation, the people who win with money are not those who know the most. They are those who do the basics, without fail, for the longest.

And while complexity may impress others, it is consistency that will quietly change your life.

Your Financial Character Is Built Daily

When people think about building wealth, they often imagine big decisions — a winning investment, a lucrative job offer, a perfectly timed market move, or a stroke of entrepreneurial luck. And while such moments can certainly accelerate financial success, they are not its foundation. The real architecture of financial well-being is not constructed through a few grand decisions, but through a multitude of small, often invisible ones. These decisions, repeated daily, shape not just your bank account — but your identity. They mold your habits, reinforce your values, and ultimately define your financial character. And like any character trait, it isn't something you are born with — it is something you build.

Character, in this context, isn't about perfection or moral superiority. It's about consistency, resilience, and alignment. It's about whether your actions reflect your stated values. It's about how you behave with money when no one is watching, when you're tired, when you're tempted, when the market is crashing or the sale is calling your name. It's about how you treat your future self in the choices you make today — and how often you choose discipline over desire, clarity over impulse, patience over panic.

Most people underestimate how much of their financial identity is shaped by the seemingly mundane moments — the decision to cook at home rather than order out, the choice to revisit a budget instead of ignoring it, the habit of checking in on your financial goals at the start of each month. These aren't dramatic acts. They won't earn praise or recognition. But they are the bricks that build the wall. And if you place enough of them, with care and intention, the structure becomes unshakable.

What's often missed in personal finance advice is that behavior doesn't just influence outcomes — it *becomes* identity. Every time you choose to act in alignment with your values — saving when it's easier to spend, investing when it's scarier to wait, planning when it's more tempting to avoid — you reinforce a belief: *this is who I am*. And that belief strengthens the habit. It creates a feedback loop. Your behavior shapes your identity, which shapes your future behavior. And over time, that loop either works for you or against you.

This is why daily actions matter so much. You don't need to overhaul your financial life in a weekend. You don't need to chase radical transformation. You just need to show up every day, in small ways, with quiet consistency. Check your accounts. Review your goals. Reflect on your spending. Make one mindful decision. One. Then repeat. Day after day. The repetition is where the magic happens. Not because it's thrilling or revolutionary — but because it's *anchoring*. It grounds you. It gives you something to hold on to when life tries to pull you off course.

There's a paradox in this truth: what feels small today ends up being the most significant over time. Big decisions feel important in the moment, but they are rare. Daily habits, on the other hand, feel insignificant — but they are relentless. And over the course of years or decades, they become the dominant force in your financial story. This is both humbling and empowering. It means you don't have to be perfect. You don't need all the answers. You just need enough self-awareness and commitment to engage with your money consistently — especially when it's boring, especially when it's uncomfortable.

Because discomfort is part of the process. Financial character is not built in moments of ease. It's forged in resistance. It's shaped in the choice to pay down debt instead of buying something new, to stay invested when the headlines are screaming panic, to walk away from a purchase that tempts your ego more than it serves your goals. These choices are not always pleasant. But they are powerful. Every time you make one, you strengthen your internal compass. You develop what some might call "money integrity" — a congruence between what you say you value and what you actually do.

And just like physical strength, financial character must be exercised. Left unattended, it atrophies. That's why daily engagement is so critical. Not obsessive, anxious engagement — but thoughtful, steady presence. A few minutes of reflection. A short journal entry about what you spent and why. A weekly check-in with your partner about shared goals. These are not tasks — they are rituals. And rituals create rhythm.

Rhythm creates identity. Identity creates destiny.

One of the biggest mistakes people make is outsourcing their financial character to external systems — to apps, algorithms, or occasional bouts of motivation. And while tools are helpful, they can't replace personal ownership. Your financial life is your responsibility. No one else can build your character for you. You can learn from others. You can adopt frameworks. But at the end of the day, you must show up for yourself. You must be the one to choose intentionality over autopilot, to ask the hard questions, to look honestly at your numbers and your narratives.

Because you are not just managing money. You are shaping the kind of person you become through your relationship with it.

Are you impulsive or intentional? Are you generous or guarded? Are you anxious or anchored? Are you chasing status or building substance?

These are not questions answered by a spreadsheet. They are answered by the stories you tell yourself — and the habits you live out.

Financial character is also about how you respond to failure. Everyone makes mistakes. Everyone overspends, forgets to save, or reacts poorly in a downturn. But character is not defined by avoidance of error — it's defined by what you do next. Do you hide from the mistake? Justify it? Repeat it? Or do you confront it with honesty, extract the lesson, and recalibrate your course? That recovery process — humble, curious, resilient — is itself a form of character development. And the more often you engage in it, the more trust you build in yourself.

Trust, after all, is the cornerstone of financial peace. Not trust in the markets, or the government, or the next big opportunity — but trust in your own ability to navigate uncertainty. Trust that you will show up for your future. Trust that you will make the next right decision, even when the last one wasn't perfect.

Trust that your financial path is not a test you can fail, but a relationship you can nurture — with patience, with presence, and with practice.

That trust doesn't come from knowledge alone. It comes from action. Repeated action. Consistent action. Daily action.

So if there's one takeaway from this subchapter, it's this: Your financial character is not something you wait to develop. It's something you cultivate — every single day — in the smallest moments, the quietest decisions, the habits no one sees. And over time, those small acts accumulate. They harden into identity. They become your foundation. And when life tests you — because it always will — it is that foundation that holds.

You don't need perfection. You don't need a master plan. You don't need to be brilliant, lucky, or born into wealth.

You just need to show up — today, tomorrow, and the day after that. One small decision at a time.

Because in the end, money doesn't just reflect your circumstances — it reflects your character. And character is built — always — in the daily choices.

Chapter 9: Enough Is a Decision, Not a Destination

In the vast landscape of financial aspiration, there is perhaps no word more powerful, more misunderstood, or more quietly radical than "enough." It is a word that lacks the flashiness of "abundance," the ambition of "more," or the romanticism of "freedom." And yet, nestled within its quiet syllables lies the most profound financial decision any person can make. To define enough is to set a boundary around desire, to draw a line that whispers, "I have reached a point where what I have no longer leaves me feeling empty." It is not a number. It is not a net worth. It is not a milestone you stumble into by accident. It is a choice — one that, once made, can radically alter the course of your financial life and your emotional well-being.

The challenge, of course, is that everything in our culture is designed to obscure that line. We live in a world where the definition of success is constantly shifting. The moment you achieve something, the target moves. A promotion once desired becomes a stepping stone to the next title. A car you once dreamed of becomes average the moment you own it. A bank balance that once felt impressive suddenly feels inadequate when you compare it to someone else's. In this game, the finish line is always running just ahead of you — close enough to see, never close enough to touch. And in chasing it, we often mistake motion for progress, consumption for success, and accumulation for meaning.

This is not just a modern dilemma. The human condition has always included a hunger for more — more security, more comfort, more recognition. It is rooted in evolution, where survival often depended on scarcity. But what once kept us alive now threatens to keep us perpetually dissatisfied. Our biology hasn't caught up with our reality. We have enough food, enough shelter, enough access — and yet, we often feel as though we're running out of time, falling behind, or missing out. Financial stress, in this light, is not always a reflection of genuine lack. Sometimes it is the symptom of having never defined what "enough" truly means to us.

That definition is where peace begins. Because the truth is, without a personal understanding of enough, no amount of financial success will feel like security. You can reach a level of wealth most would envy — and still lie awake at night worrying about losing it, about whether it's truly "enough," about whether someone else has more. The problem isn't the amount. It's the absence of a boundary. It's the illusion that the next zero in your account will finally quiet the noise inside you, only to discover it merely raises the volume.

What's even more insidious is that in a world obsessed with growth, saying "enough" can feel like failure. If you stop striving, aren't you settling? If you're content, aren't you giving up? This cultural myth — that fulfillment is complacency — drives countless people into endless cycles of work, worry, and wanting. It turns ambition into addiction. And like any addiction, the high wears off quickly, leaving only the need for another hit.

But "enough" isn't a lack of ambition. It's the ultimate expression of self-awareness. It's the realization that success isn't a number on a screen but a state of being. It's understanding that joy, meaning, and freedom aren't purchased at the store or unlocked with a six-figure salary. They are cultivated — often through simplicity, intentionality, and the courage to step off the treadmill of comparison.

To define enough is to reclaim agency. It allows you to spend, save, invest, and give with clarity rather than confusion. It lets you say yes to what matters and no to what merely looks impressive. It frees you from the toxic belief that more is always better — and replaces it with the healthier, braver belief that *better is better*, and better is often quieter, slower, and smaller than we've been taught to believe.

More importantly, enough is not just a financial concept — it's a psychological and spiritual one. It's about alignment. When your desires align with your reality, you experience peace. When your expectations align with your actions, you experience power. And when your sense of worth is no longer tethered to accumulation, you experience freedom. But none of these are possible if you allow the definition of enough to be outsourced — to your peers, your feed, or the flashing metrics of consumer culture.

This chapter is about that process — not the arrival at enough, but the decision to define it. Because make no mistake: it is a decision. No one hands it to you. No amount of income guarantees it. No financial advisor can prescribe it. You have to choose it. You have to say, with quiet authority, "This is sufficient for me. I don't need more to matter. I don't need more to feel safe. I don't need more to belong." That choice is not easy. It will be tested daily. But it is also the foundation upon which true financial well-being is built.

In the pages that follow, we'll explore why satisfaction is such a moving target (and how to stabilize it), why the chase for more rarely ends in peace, how to define enough on your own terms, how contentment becomes a competitive advantage in both life and money, and why true wealth often looks less like opulence and more like inner stillness. These are not easy topics. They cut to the heart of what we believe about value, success, and identity. But they are necessary. Because until you define enough, every financial decision will be haunted by uncertainty — not of numbers, but of purpose.

And so, this chapter is not just an invitation. It's a challenge. To pause. To reflect. To ask questions that most financial advice skips over. What are you really working for? When will it be enough? And if you never define that — how will you know when you've arrived?

You might discover that the finish line was never ahead of you. It was always within.

The Moving Goalpost of Satisfaction

There's a particular kind of exhaustion that creeps in—not after a period of loss, but after a moment of gain. A strange, hollow feeling that emerges in the silence following a long-awaited achievement. You arrive. You get what you wanted. You hold it in your hands, see it in your account, drive it down the road, maybe even wear it on your wrist. And then, almost imperceptibly at first, the satisfaction begins to fade. What once lit you up now feels... ordinary. What once seemed like enough now looks like the baseline. The goalpost has moved. Again. And it's in this subtle but relentless shift that so much of modern financial stress is born—not from not having, but from never feeling like what we do have is enough for long.

Satisfaction, we're told, is the reward for effort. It's the light at the end of the tunnel. But the truth is far less linear. In reality, satisfaction is slippery, evasive, and often psychological. It's not found in numbers, but in narratives. Not in outcomes, but in outlook. And perhaps most painfully, it's not always proportional to how hard we've worked or how far we've come. In fact, some of the most dissatisfied people are those who have achieved the most—because the more they get, the more they feel they must maintain, the more they fear losing, and the more they realize that arrival never actually brings the peace they imagined.

This is the cruel trick of the moving goalpost. It feeds on progress. It uses your growth against you. What once thrilled you now bores you, because your baseline has shifted. What once felt extravagant now feels standard. And as the context of your life changes, so does your reference point. This is called hedonic adaptation—the psychological phenomenon where people quickly return to a relatively stable level of happiness despite major positive or negative events. You thought the raise, the car, the milestone would make you feel secure, worthy, validated. And it did—briefly. But then your mind adjusted. And now you're right back where you started, except the bar is higher.

Consider how this plays out over a lifetime. In your early career, a modest paycheck feels like freedom. You imagine that if you ever made double, you'd never complain again. Fast forward a few years, and you're making twice that amount—but you're also spending more, comparing more, and somehow feeling more financially anxious than ever. The numbers have changed, but the story hasn't. Because the story is driven by relative satisfaction, not absolute achievement. And relative satisfaction is always at the mercy of context: who you're around, what you're exposed to, what your peers have, and what the culture tells you is normal.

That's why social comparison is such a powerful fuel for dissatisfaction. You could be living a life of abundance, comfort, and opportunity—and feel poor the moment you scroll through a curated feed of someone else's "better" life. This isn't immaturity; it's human nature. We are wired to measure ourselves against others, especially those we perceive to be in our reference group. But what we forget is that everyone is playing a different game, with different rules, risks, and responsibilities. And yet, we borrow their scorecards and use them to judge our own lives. The result? Chronic dissatisfaction, even in the midst of real success.

The moving goalpost also disguises itself as ambition. "I just want to grow," we say. "I'm not greedy, I'm driven." And while growth is not inherently bad, it becomes problematic when it's untethered from purpose. When you chase more because more is all you've been taught to chase, you lose touch with what you actually want. You get caught in a loop of striving, achieving, adjusting, and striving again. You never pause long enough to ask, "What would enough look like—for me?" Because in the race toward the next thing, reflection feels like a delay. Stillness feels like failure.

But the deeper truth is this: satisfaction isn't the result of having more. It's the result of wanting less—or at least wanting intentionally. When you don't define your own goalpost, the world will define it for you. And the world's version will always be just out of reach. It's designed that way. Modern capitalism depends on dissatisfaction. Entire industries exist to remind you of what you lack, of how behind you are, of what you still "need" to be whole. It's a machine fueled by moving goalposts, and if you don't step off the track occasionally, you will spend your entire life running after things that were never meant to bring lasting joy in the first place.

So what's the alternative? It's not apathy. It's not rejecting growth or ambition or financial goals. It's discernment. It's the practice of naming your own enough—before the world does. It's regularly revisiting your desires, not to kill them, but to understand them. To ask: Where is this coming from? Is this mine, or was it planted by someone else? Does this want align with my values, or just my ego? It's a willingness to slow down and notice that satisfaction is not something you can chase—it's something you can cultivate, often in quiet, grounded ways.

One of the most powerful financial practices you can adopt is a simple ritual of gratitude and reflection. Not performative gratitude. Not toxic positivity. But a real, honest accounting of what you already have, what it already gives you, and whether the next rung on the ladder is truly necessary—or just familiar.

When you take stock of your life through this lens, you begin to see how much of your dissatisfaction has little to do with actual lack, and everything to do with shifting standards and invisible comparisons.

You also begin to realize that satisfaction doesn't require perfection. You can be content and still have goals. You can feel grateful and still desire change. The difference lies in the emotional posture: one is rooted in lack, the other in sufficiency. One says, "I won't be happy until…" The other says, "I am grounded now, even as I grow." The former keeps you chasing. The latter lets you rest, even as you move forward.

There's also wisdom in recognizing that goalposts will always shift—it's part of human nature. But what you can control is how you respond. You can catch yourself mid-chase and pause. You can notice the reflex and choose differently. You can remind yourself that every time you arrive at a new level, the view changes—but that doesn't mean your values have to. In fact, holding onto your values in the face of shifting standards is one of the most radical forms of financial clarity you can develop.

Think of the people in your life who seem most at peace with their finances. They're not always the wealthiest. They're the ones who have decided what matters—and live accordingly. They spend in ways that reflect their priorities, not just their income. They don't get swept up in status games because they've opted out of that particular scoreboard. They're not immune to desire or ambition—but they are anchored. They know where their goalpost is, and they revisit it often.

That's what this subchapter is really about: awareness. Awareness of the psychological forces that shape your sense of satisfaction. Awareness of the cultural scripts that define success. Awareness of your own shifting standards, and the courage to pause and recalibrate when needed. Because without that awareness, you are a passenger on someone else's journey—moving fast, but never arriving.

So pause now, wherever you are in your financial life, and ask: When was the last time I felt truly satisfied? What was present in that moment? What was absent? And am I still chasing that feeling—or something the world told me I should want instead?

Satisfaction is not a permanent state. It comes and goes. But it becomes more accessible, more stable, and more meaningful when you realize it isn't waiting for you somewhere far ahead.

It's right here—if you're willing to stop, look around, and decide that, at least for this moment, you are already enough.

Why Chasing More Never Ends

The pursuit of "more" is one of the most persistent, seductive, and socially sanctioned obsessions of the modern age. It disguises itself as ambition, as progress, as a hunger for excellence. It wears the mask of drive, of discipline, of the entrepreneurial spirit. It whispers encouragement in the language of success and self-improvement. But beneath the polished exterior, "more" has a darker truth: it is a destination that does not exist. It is a road with no finish line, a game with no rules, a hunger that cannot be fed. And when left unchecked, it becomes not a path to fulfillment — but a treadmill of dissatisfaction that speeds up the closer we believe we are to winning.

Why is chasing more so addictive? Because it plays on the deepest layers of human psychology — our fear of scarcity, our need for significance, our desire to feel safe, respected, and worthy. From childhood, we're conditioned to believe that the answer to insecurity is addition. Add degrees, titles, square footage, salary digits, Instagram likes. Accumulate, acquire, achieve. Because more, we are told, equals better. More means you're doing well. More means you matter.

And for a while, it works. You get the promotion, and you feel competent. You buy the new car, and you feel successful. You earn the bigger paycheck, and you feel secure. But the high fades fast — because the baseline shifts. Your expectations expand to match your new reality. What once was a dream becomes standard, even expected. And the bar moves — subtly, silently — until what once satisfied you no longer registers as special.

This phenomenon has a name: the hedonic treadmill. It's the psychological mechanism by which we adapt quickly to improvements in our lives, only to return to our emotional baseline and crave the next upgrade. The treadmill doesn't slow down. It doesn't stop. It simply resets the incline — and asks you to keep running. And the more you earn, achieve, or consume without conscious reflection, the faster the belt turns beneath your feet.

The cruel irony of the hedonic treadmill is that it rewards effort with emptiness. You reach your goal, only to find it wasn't the goal at all. So you pick a new one. And the cycle begins again. You tell yourself the next level will be different — that once you hit six figures, or seven, or retire early, or buy that dream home, then you'll feel whole. But satisfaction, it turns out, doesn't live in the numbers. It lives in your relationship to the numbers. And if that relationship is built on fear, comparison, or scarcity, no amount will ever be enough.

One of the most dangerous myths in personal finance and business culture is that there is a magic threshold where "more" becomes unnecessary — that once you cross a certain income or asset level, you'll automatically feel content. But money doesn't change your emotional wiring. It amplifies it. If you were anxious at $50,000, you might be anxious at $500,000 — just with fancier problems. If you were constantly comparing yourself to peers at one level, you'll find new peers, with higher benchmarks, at the next. And so the chase continues, not because of need, but because of inertia. Because stopping feels like quitting.

Because slowing down feels like failure.

This isn't a call to reject growth or ambition. Wanting more is not inherently wrong. It becomes destructive only when it's unexamined — when the desire for more is not tied to purpose, but to reflex. When it's driven by fear rather than clarity. When we seek more not because it adds to our life, but because we've never learned how to be at peace with what we have.

To escape the trap of endless chasing, we must first ask: what is the emotional promise that "more" is making to us? Is it security? Approval? Control? Freedom? Most often, it is not the object itself we crave

— but the feeling we hope it will give us. And once we identify that feeling, we can begin to question whether "more" is actually the only — or best — path to get there. Because often, the answer is no.

Security, for example, is not a number — it is a mindset. It comes not from how much you have, but from how little you need. Approval is not earned through possessions — it is granted by those who love you as you are. Control is not found in financial domination — it is found in emotional regulation and clarity of purpose. And freedom? It often has less to do with assets and more to do with your willingness to say "no" — to obligations, to pressures, to other people's expectations of what your life should look like.

Another reason chasing more never ends is that it becomes entangled with identity. We begin to define ourselves by what we have or do — by the size of our portfolio, the brand of our clothes, the prestige of our job title. And once our identity is built on these fragile foundations, letting go feels like erasure.

Scaling back feels like disappearing. We cling to "more" not because we need it, but because we fear who we might be without it.

This is why one of the most courageous financial moves you can make is not to earn more — but to want less. To consciously choose sufficiency over scarcity. To decouple your identity from your income. To measure your worth not by accumulation, but by alignment. To pause and ask, "Who am I becoming in the pursuit of more? And is that who I want to be?"

Because make no mistake — every dollar you chase comes with an invisible cost. The cost of time, of energy, of presence. The cost of relationships neglected, of values compromised, of peace postponed. More money can buy you many things, but it cannot buy you back the years you spent too busy to enjoy what you already had. It cannot refund the birthdays missed, the evenings glued to a screen, the anxiety carried like a second skin.

True financial freedom, then, is not just having more. It is needing less. It is standing in a world that screams "upgrade!" and whispering back, "I'm good." It is recognizing that wealth is not defined by what you accumulate — but by how little you need to feel whole.

Of course, this is easier said than done. The world rewards performance. Social media celebrates excess. Productivity culture glorifies burnout. But the decision to exit the rat race — even partially — is an act of quiet rebellion. It is the choice to live by your own metrics. To seek progress, not perfection. To define success on your own terms, not someone else's highlight reel.

It's worth asking yourself: what am I chasing, and why? What story am I believing about what happens when I finally arrive? And what if that story isn't true?

Because more will never end. There is always another level, another competitor, another goal. But your time is finite. Your energy is precious. Your joy is not a renewable resource if it is constantly postponed. At some point, you must choose: do I keep chasing the horizon, or do I plant my feet and enjoy the view from here?

That doesn't mean you stop dreaming. It means you learn to anchor your dreams in presence. It means you allow yourself to feel satisfied before the next milestone. It means you measure success not just by growth, but by gratitude.

Because more isn't wrong — but it's never enough on its own. And until you realize that, it will own you. It will drive you. It will steal from you. And it will never stop asking for more.

But you can stop. You can step off the treadmill. You can choose clarity over compulsion. You can decide

— today — that your worth is not up for auction, and your life is not a performance. You are already enough.

And once you truly believe that, you'll see: the chase ends when you say it does.

Defining "Enough" on Your Terms

There is a particular kind of power—quiet, unshakable, and deeply personal—that comes from defining what "enough" means to you. It is not the kind of power you can broadcast or flaunt. You won't see it on a financial statement or in a trophy case. But it manifests in the calm with which you make decisions, the steadiness with which you move through your days, and the confidence with which you say "no" to things that once ruled you. Defining enough is, in essence, reclaiming authorship over your own life story— choosing not just how the story ends, but what it's about in the first place.

And yet, for something so essential to our well-being, so central to our emotional and financial health, we rarely pause to define it. Most people inherit their sense of "enough" from the world around them—from family expectations, peer comparisons, social media narratives, or cultural scripts that equate more with better. We chase after bigger homes, higher salaries, and more elaborate lifestyles not because we've sat down and determined that those things are integral to our well-being, but because we assume that's what success looks like. That's what winning means. That's what we're supposed to want.

But what if that story doesn't fit you? What if, buried beneath all the noise of comparison and ambition, your definition of enough is radically simpler, gentler, or more aligned with a different kind of richness— one that can't be measured in dollars?

The act of defining enough begins with awareness—specifically, awareness of how your current definition was formed. Who taught you what success looks like? Who told you what matters? What messages about money, worth, and identity did you internalize as truth without ever questioning them? The stories we carry—often inherited, sometimes unspoken—have enormous power over our behaviors. But they lose their grip the moment we bring them into the light. And it is only through that examination that we can begin to write a story that is truly our own.

Consider, for example, the difference between goals driven by ego and goals rooted in values. The former often come from comparison: "They have it, so I should too." The latter come from clarity: "This matters to me, even if no one sees it." When we define enough through ego, it becomes a moving target. When we define it through values, it becomes a compass.

This is why so many people feel unfulfilled despite achieving impressive financial success—because they never defined success for themselves. They outsourced that definition to culture, only to discover that it brought achievement but not alignment. They reached the summit of someone else's mountain. And they're left wondering why the view doesn't bring peace.

To define enough on your terms, you must ask questions that cut beneath the surface of desire. Not just "What do I want?" but "Why do I want it?" Not just "How much is enough?" but "Enough for what?" For security? For freedom? For time with family? For peace of mind? For creative expression? When you connect your financial goals to emotional outcomes, you begin to see that money is never the point—it's the tool. And like any tool, its value lies in how effectively it helps you build what you truly care about.

This clarity becomes especially important in a world obsessed with optimization. We are constantly told that we should be doing more, earning more, investing smarter, retiring earlier. There is always a next level. But optimization without intention is a trap. It keeps you busy, but not fulfilled. Productive, but not purposeful. By defining enough, you give yourself permission to stop climbing when the view is beautiful, not just when you've reached the top.

That doesn't mean settling. It means being strategic. It means recognizing that every dollar, every hour, every ounce of energy has an opportunity cost. When you say yes to more work, what are you saying no to? When you say yes to a bigger home, what are you saying no to in terms of flexibility, freedom, or time? The moment you define what enough looks like, you also begin to see what isn't worth the trade.

Let's ground this in practical terms. For some, enough might mean a modest home, a predictable schedule, and the ability to be home for dinner every night. For others, it might mean building a business they believe in, even if it never scales to millions. For someone else, enough could be the ability to travel a few times a year, support a cause they care about, or live without debt. There is no universal template. The definition of enough must be handcrafted—not copied, not imposed.

And that definition isn't static. It should evolve with your life. What felt like enough in your twenties may not serve you in your forties. Parenthood, health, loss, growth—these experiences reshape what matters. But the key is that you continue to ask. You revisit the question: "Is this still enough? And if not, what is?" Because failing to ask that question is how people end up in lives that look good on paper but feel empty in practice.

It's also how people end up financially overextended—chasing a lifestyle that doesn't actually align with their priorities. When you define enough, you gain not just emotional clarity, but financial discipline. You stop spending reflexively. You stop buying for approval. You stop chasing upgrades you don't need. And instead, you begin to allocate resources toward what actually brings joy, meaning, and peace.

One of the most liberating aspects of defining enough is that it allows you to opt out of the comparison game. You no longer need to keep up with anyone else because your definition isn't theirs. You're not playing the same game. Their highlight reel becomes irrelevant to your quiet contentment. And that, in today's hyper-comparative world, is a kind of superpower.

But perhaps the most beautiful result of defining enough is that it opens space for gratitude. When you know what is sufficient, you can fully appreciate what you already have. You can savor the present, rather than constantly reaching for the future. You can feel rich—not because you have everything, but because you've decided that what you have is enough.

Gratitude is not complacency. It's not a passive surrender to mediocrity. It's an active acknowledgment of sufficiency. It's a refusal to let desire steal your presence. And it's only possible when you draw a line— when you say, "This is what I need. This is what serves me. This is what matters." Everything beyond that is optional, not essential. A bonus, not a requirement.

Defining enough on your terms will not exempt you from the pressures of the world. You'll still see the ads. You'll still hear the bragging. You'll still feel the occasional pull of "what if." But you'll have an anchor. You'll have a reference point that is rooted in truth, not trend. And that anchor will help you make better decisions—not just financially, but emotionally.

Because at the end of the day, money is a means. The destination is meaning. And the only way to reach that destination is to know when to stop chasing, when to start enjoying, and when to say, with quiet conviction: "This, right here, is enough. For me. Today. On my terms." And in that moment, you will have claimed something far rarer than wealth. You will have claimed peace.

Contentment as a Competitive Advantage

In a world that runs on restlessness, where the engines of economy, technology, and culture are fueled by the never-ending promise of the next upgrade, the next milestone, the next win—it might seem strange, even counterintuitive, to talk about contentment as a form of advantage. After all, contentment is quiet. It is still. It does not shout its presence or parade its accomplishments. But perhaps that is exactly where its power lies: in its refusal to be pulled into the noisy arms race of perpetual dissatisfaction. In a system where everyone is running, not always toward something, but more often away from the fear of not being enough, the person who is at peace with what they have—who chooses to build a life around sufficiency rather than scarcity—moves differently. They play a different game. And they win in ways that go unnoticed on spreadsheets, but felt deeply in their health, their time, their relationships, and their sanity.

To understand contentment as a competitive advantage, you first have to recognize what most people are competing for. In a traditional sense, the race is toward accumulation—more money, more status, more followers, more proof of success. And while there is nothing inherently wrong with any of these pursuits, they often come bundled with invisible costs. The cost of time, the cost of attention, the cost of constantly comparing yourself to others. The irony is that many people enter the race seeking freedom, only to find themselves trapped by the very rewards they were chasing. A bigger paycheck comes with a bigger role, a bigger role with bigger stress, and soon, the person who once dreamed of liberation becomes enslaved to maintaining an image they never paused to question.

Contentment breaks that cycle. It is not the absence of ambition, but the presence of clarity. It is the deep inner knowing that you have what you need—and that needing less from the world is often the most liberating form of wealth. A content person is not stagnant; they grow, they build, they dream—but they are not driven by the ache of emptiness or the fear of inadequacy. They are driven by purpose, by alignment, by the quiet satisfaction of progress that is meaningful, not performative.

And in a world where attention is scarce and distraction is endless, this kind of clarity is an advantage. It means you spend less time chasing validation and more time creating value. Less time managing impressions and more time deepening your mastery. While others are exhausted by the constant demands of keeping up, you are energized by the freedom of staying grounded. Contentment doesn't slow you down—it focuses you. It allows you to say no to what doesn't serve you, and yes to what does, even if no one else is watching.

One of the most overlooked benefits of contentment is its ability to protect your energy. Most people underestimate how much energy is lost to comparison—to scrolling through social media feeds and recalibrating their self-worth based on curated snapshots of other people's lives. But the content person opts out of that cycle. They don't need to measure their progress against someone else's highlight reel. They don't need to constantly prove themselves. And in doing so, they recover time, focus, and emotional bandwidth that others unknowingly squander.

This translates into better decisions. In finance, business, and life, poor decisions are often made not from ignorance, but from pressure—pressure to act quickly, to outperform, to outshine. But a content person has nothing to prove. They can afford to be patient. They can afford to think long-term. They're not reactive. They're not impulsive. And in an economy that rewards clarity, that kind of measured thinking is a serious edge.

Contentment also brings an often-forgotten form of resilience: the ability to remain steady when others are thrown off course. When markets crash, when peers surge ahead, when the game changes—those who have anchored their worth in external validation are shaken. But those who are content are grounded.

They don't crumble because their foundation was never built on appearances. Their sense of success was never dependent on what other people thought. This kind of inner sturdiness cannot be bought or borrowed. It is cultivated, slowly, through the daily decision to define enough and stand by it.

There's also an economic advantage to contentment. People who are content tend to spend less—not because they're frugal or deprived, but because they're not trying to fill an emotional void with material things. They buy with intention. They invest with purpose. They don't fall for every marketing message because they're not constantly trying to signal their worth. As a result, they save more, they build wealth more sustainably, and they often reach financial independence faster—not because they make more, but because they need less to feel whole.

This doesn't mean content people never spend or indulge. It means they do so from a place of joy, not compulsion. From alignment, not anxiety. There's a big difference between spending money to enhance your life and spending money to escape your life. Content people know the difference. And that awareness creates space for financial decisions that are not only wiser, but more satisfying.

In relationships, contentment also proves itself as a strength. When you're not constantly chasing the next thing, you become more present. You listen better. You show up more fully. You're not distracted by your to-do list or consumed by your next milestone. You're able to engage deeply with the people around you— not as a means to an end, but as an end in itself. This depth of presence builds trust, connection, and intimacy in ways that no amount of professional success ever could.

And in leadership, whether in business or community, contentment is magnetic. People trust leaders who are calm, grounded, and emotionally secure. They follow those who radiate enoughness—not arrogance, not scarcity, but a quiet confidence that says, "I'm not here to prove anything. I'm here to build something meaningful." That kind of presence creates safety. It invites collaboration. It reduces drama. And in a world overflowing with noisy, insecure leaders chasing the next high, the content leader stands out—not because they're louder, but because they're rooted.

It's important to clarify, again, that contentment is not the same as complacency. Complacency is stagnation. It's a refusal to grow, to learn, to stretch. Contentment, on the other hand, is an invitation to grow from a place of peace. It says, "I am enough—and still, I can become more." It's the difference between striving from lack and growing from love. Between chasing out of fear and creating out of vision.

So how do you cultivate this kind of contentment? It begins with noticing where you've outsourced your definition of success. Where are you still playing someone else's game? Whose approval are you still seeking? What milestones are you chasing, not because they matter to you, but because they signal status to someone else?

Then, slowly, you begin the process of detaching. You define enough. You choose your values. You create rituals of gratitude and reflection. You build a life that feels good on the inside, even if it doesn't always look impressive from the outside. And over time, you begin to feel the difference—not just in your mood, but in your momentum. You move with clarity. You choose with confidence. You live with less noise.

In a world where everyone is sprinting toward a finish line that keeps moving, contentment allows you to walk—deliberately, purposefully, with your head held high. You don't need to win the race. Because you've realized: the real victory was stepping off the track entirely.

Contentment is not a withdrawal from ambition. It is its evolution. It is ambition reimagined—not as a desperate climb toward validation, but as a quiet commitment to live well, love deeply, and create from a place of wholeness. And in a world addicted to more, there is no greater competitive advantage than the radical, revolutionary act of being truly, completely, joyfully content.

The Wealth of Peace vs. The Price of Comparison

There is a kind of wealth that doesn't show up in bank accounts or asset reports—a wealth that cannot be deposited, withdrawn, or taxed. It is not made of currency, but of calm. Not measured in net worth, but in emotional balance. It is the wealth of peace. And in a culture that constantly urges us to run faster, climb higher, and do more, it is perhaps the most underappreciated and undervalued form of prosperity. Because while many chase the illusion of security through accumulation, very few stop to ask whether peace might offer something even more enduring: a life that feels complete even when it doesn't look extraordinary. A life that no longer needs to be compared to be worthy.

Comparison is the silent thief of peace. It does not knock loudly or announce its arrival. It slips in quietly, often disguised as harmless observation—scrolling through someone else's vacation photos, reading about a colleague's promotion, noticing the newer car in your neighbor's driveway. But beneath the surface of those small glances, something dangerous stirs: the subtle suggestion that your life, as it stands now, is insufficient. That someone else has figured out something you haven't. That happiness, fulfillment, or success must exist elsewhere—in another person's house, career, body, or bank account.

And once comparison takes root, it does not stay confined. It spreads—fast and wide. It infiltrates the way you measure progress, the way you interpret your self-worth, the way you set your goals. It rewrites your story with someone else's ink. You no longer ask, "What do I truly want?" Instead, you ask, "What do they have that I don't?" And from that question, discontent blooms.

The price of comparison is rarely calculated in dollars, but it is expensive nonetheless. It costs you your gratitude. It diminishes your joy. It poisons your motivation—not with ambition, but with anxiety. You may still achieve your goals, but the process feels heavier, the satisfaction more fleeting. Because no matter how well you do, there is always someone doing better. And when your self-worth is tethered to someone else's trajectory, peace becomes impossible.

This is where the true poverty of comparison reveals itself. It is not that you lack resources—it is that you lack rest. You lie awake at night replaying what you should have done differently, obsessing over someone else's timeline, wondering if your path is valid simply because it isn't identical to theirs. You stop trusting your instincts. You second-guess your choices. And in doing so, you trade the richness of your unique journey for the illusion of catching up to someone else's.

The irony, of course, is that comparison rarely gives you the whole picture. You're measuring your internal reality against someone else's external highlight reel. You see their curated moments, not their quiet battles. Their celebrations, not their sacrifices. You don't see the fear behind their ambition, the loneliness beneath their success, the compromises they've made to get where they are. And yet, without this context, you assume they must be happier, wiser, more complete. So you chase an image—not a truth.

Peace, by contrast, doesn't chase. It chooses. It says: I do not need to be better than anyone else. I only need to be aligned with myself. Peace is found not in achieving more, but in needing less validation. Not in being the best, but in being enough. It is not passive resignation—it is active clarity. It is the decision to live from the inside out, rather than the outside in.

There is profound strength in this choice. In a world where identity is often built on status and performance, the person who anchors their worth in inner steadiness becomes unshakable. They don't collapse when someone else succeeds. They don't crumble under the weight of comparison. They cheer for others without questioning their own path. They know that success is not a zero-sum game. That someone else's rise is not their fall. That life is not a race—it's a practice.

And that practice requires boundaries. Because the platforms we inhabit—social media, career networks, news feeds—are designed to keep us watching, scrolling, measuring. They amplify comparison by design. And if we're not careful, we begin to curate our own lives for others rather than living them for ourselves. We perform joy instead of experiencing it. We share our wins to feel worthy instead of simply feeling proud. And slowly, we forget what it felt like to move through life without constantly asking, "How do I compare?"

To reclaim peace, we must begin with presence. We must return to our own lane. We must ask deeper questions: What truly matters to me? What am I grateful for right now? What does a good life feel like— not look like? Because peace cannot be purchased, but it can be practiced. It begins in the small choices— turning off the screen, stepping outside, taking a breath, writing a journal entry, speaking kindly to yourself. These are not glamorous actions. But they are revolutionary in a world that profits off your insecurity.

Another powerful antidote to comparison is self-compassion. We often judge ourselves more harshly than we ever would others. We expect progress without setbacks, growth without doubt, success without delay. But peace grows when we offer ourselves the grace to be human—messy, evolving, imperfect. When we stop asking ourselves to be extraordinary and instead ask, "Am I being honest? Am I being true?" Peace lives in that honesty.

And it expands when we connect with others not through competition, but through authenticity. When we drop the performance and speak from our real experiences. When we say, "I don't have it all figured out, but I'm doing my best." Those are the moments when comparison dissolves and connection begins.

Because the truth is, everyone is carrying something. No one is as polished as they seem. And the more we open ourselves to real conversation, the less power comparison has over us.

Peace also flourishes in simplicity. When you strip away the excess—financial, emotional, mental—you begin to see how little you actually need to feel whole. It's not the accumulation of options that brings freedom; often, it's the reduction of noise. When your values are clear, your decisions become easier. When your needs are grounded, your spending becomes intentional. When your self-worth is no longer for sale, your energy returns to you. And that, truly, is wealth.

Because peace is the ultimate ROI. It's the return on a life lived in alignment. It's the yield of boundaries honored, of values practiced, of enough declared. It's waking up and not needing to impress anyone. It's falling asleep without the weight of comparison pressing on your chest. It's a clear mind. A steady heart. A life that feels good from the inside.

That is wealth.

And it's available—not someday, not once you've achieved some arbitrary goal—but right now, in this moment, if you're willing to let go of the measuring stick and come back to yourself.

So ask yourself: What is the cost of comparison in my life? What does it steal from me—time, energy, joy? And what would it look like to release it—not completely, but just enough to breathe again? Enough to reclaim your own story, your own voice, your own values?

Because you don't need to win a race you never chose. You don't need to match a pace that was never yours. And you certainly don't need to become someone else to feel whole.

You are already enough.

And the moment you truly believe that, you will feel the kind of wealth that no amount of money can buy: the unshakable, undeniable, incomparable wealth of peace.

Chapter 10: Behavior Is the True Asset

For decades, we have been taught that the path to financial success lies in uncovering the right strategy, mastering the correct formulas, and outsmarting the market or the next person in line. We pore over annualized returns, back-test models, compare fees, and debate which economic indicators portend the next cycle. We believe that if we only find the perfect algorithm or the hottest tip, we will unlock the door to lasting wealth. And yet, time and again, history shows us that the most brilliant plans suffer when the people behind them buckle under the weight of fear, greed, impatience, or overconfidence. The most meticulously researched portfolio collapses when its manager panics at the first sign of a downturn. The most carefully considered budget unravels when overspending is easier than resisting temptation on an exhausting week. The most brilliant entrepreneur falters if they cannot adapt when their confidence clouds their judgment.

This truth reveals itself in every financial crisis, every personal story of near-miss regret, and every high-flyer who burns out at the peak of success. It's not that strategy doesn't matter; it's that strategy is nothing without behavior. And behavior—how we act, how we feel, how we respond to uncertainty, how we manage our impulses—is the true, enduring asset in any financial endeavor. In other words, the capital you invest in understanding, shaping, and strengthening your own behavioral response to money is worth far more than any market position you could ever take.

The painful irony is that behavior is the one factor we overlook most often. We stock our minds with knowledge, soak up advice, and optimize theories. We hire planners, use advanced software, and subscribe to premium insights. But when it comes to the real work—learning to calm our panic when the market dips, restraining our urge to chase the next hot trend, showing patience when results are slow—we shrug and say, "I'll get better." We leave our most important asset—ourselves—undisciplined, untrained, and at the mercy of every emotional fad that comes our way.

Imagine two investors: one who spends hours studying economic data but panics and pulls out when the market slips five percent; the other who barely knows the details but has practiced emotional resilience, stayed put through multiple cycles, and reaped steady returns. Which one is truly in control of their financial destiny? The answer is obvious. Knowledge without the emotional fortitude to apply it consistently is like having a high-performance car with no brakes. You can speed ahead, but a small error will end in a crash.

Behavioral wealth-building is about building your own brakes—and your own steering. It's about cultivating the mindset, habits, and resilience that allow you to deploy strategy without being ruled by momentary impulses. It's about training yourself to see beyond immediate discomfort and to make decisions aligned with your long-term goals, even when your emotions scream for a quick fix, a momentary high, or an escape from anxiety.

Yet this work cannot be outsourced. No amount of software can edit your emotional response. No advisor can live inside your head. No algorithm can feel your fear or resist your urge to sell low and buy high. If you want to succeed over the long haul, you must invest in your own capacity to handle adversity, stay curious when certainty vanishes, and remain humble when success arrives. You must learn to manage your attention—knowing what to ignore in a world of noise—and to cultivate self-awareness, the foundation upon which every wise decision rests.

This chapter is an invitation—and a challenge—to shift your focus from the external mechanics of finance to the internal work of character. We will explore how seeing yourself as the primary investment changes the way you allocate time, attention, and resources. We will delve into the art of emotional resilience, learning how to stay balanced amid volatility rather than react to it. We will revisit the concept of long- term thinking, but not as a lofty ideal; as a practical discipline in a world designed to tug you toward instant gratification. We will discover why self-awareness—understanding your own tendencies, biases, and blind spots—is a more powerful tool than any chart or metric. And we will conclude by showing how your financial future is shaped less by what you own today and more by who you become through the choices you make each day.

Because at the end of the day, markets will rise and fall, interest rates will fluctuate, and new investment vehicles will emerge. But your ability to show up—calm, clear-headed, and committed—through all of it is the true asset that compounds over time. Your behavior is the only strategy you can rely on when everything else changes. And it is the one thing no one can take away from you.

So let us turn inward, and begin building the most important portfolio you will ever manage: the portfolio of your own behavior.

You Are the Investment

When we talk about assets, we instinctively picture tangible things: stocks, bonds, real estate, businesses, ventures—line items on a balance sheet that can be bought, sold, valued, or leveraged. Yet, if you peer behind the veneer of every financial statement, you will find the same underlying truth: your most critical asset is you. Not your portfolio, not your car or your house, not even the intellectual property you own. It is your mind, your character, your attention, your resilience, and your capacity to learn, adapt, and persevere. Because no strategy, no matter how brilliant on paper, can be executed without the person executing it. And that person—you—must be cultivated with as much intention, rigor, and patience as any other asset you hold.

To think of yourself as the primary investment requires a seismic shift in perspective. Instead of asking, "What should I invest in?" the more fundamental question becomes, "How should I invest in myself?" This reframing opens a world of possibilities: investing in your emotional intelligence, your capacity to manage fear and greed; in your habits of discipline and consistency; in your health, energy, and stress resilience; in your ability to delay gratification and think long term. These investments rarely appear on a spreadsheet or in a quarterly report. They don't generate quarterly dividends or capital gains. Yet, over time, they compound in ways that far outstrip market returns, because they shape the very quality of every decision you make.

Consider the person who invests not just money, but time and attention into developing emotional resilience. They read widely about cognitive biases, practice mindfulness to observe their impulses, cultivate routines that anchor them in calm during market volatility, and seek out mentors or peers who challenge their assumptions. These efforts don't pay off immediately—in fact, they often feel like a distraction from more "productive" tasks. But when the next downturn arrives, when fear asks you to sell low, when herd mentality screams that you should panic, your emotional investment pays dividends. You stay calm. You remember your principles. You avoid rash moves and benefit from the rebound that follows. Your portfolio may have fallen 30 percent, but your confidence falls zero.

Or consider the investment in self-discipline: automating savings, setting rigid boundaries around lifestyle inflation, creating friction for impulsive spending, building systems that remove willpower from routine choices. These steps may seem small or mundane. But each act of restraint, repeated over months and years, frees capital for higher-priority uses and protects you from the slow leak of lifestyle creep. More importantly, they reinforce an identity: "I am the kind of person who follows through." And that identity

—once its roots run deep—acts as a self-fulfilling prophecy, guiding choices toward long-term wealth rather than short-term gratification.

Investing in knowledge is often celebrated, but the deeper investment is in *applied* knowledge. Learning about compound interest, the psychology of risk, or tax efficiency is valuable—but worthless unless you apply it consistently. The gap between knowing and doing is where most of us fail. The person who reads one book on investing but never opens an account gains no financial return. But the person who automates a modest monthly contribution, even without deep theoretical understanding, begins to build wealth. That action—the behavioral application of knowledge—is the real investment.

Your health, too, is an asset. Chronic stress, poor sleep, and low energy degrade your ability to think clearly, manage risk, and sustain the long-term focus that wealth-building demands. One of the highest returns you can earn is on sleep, nutrition, exercise, and stress management. These are not luxury expenses; they are foundational investments in your capacity to make sound financial decisions, weather uncertainty, and maintain the discipline required to stay the course.

Similarly, investing in relationships—family, friends, mentors, advisors—builds both emotional support and intellectual capital. A financial plan is only as good as the person executing it, and execution often breaks down in isolation. When you commit to regular conversations with trusted confidants, seek honest feedback, and build a network that challenges you, you strengthen your own resolve. You see blind spots you couldn't see alone. You resist groupthink. You benefit from collective wisdom. These relational investments are seldom quantified, but they are life—and portfolio—saving.

Most importantly, investing in yourself means embracing a growth mindset. Believing that your abilities, intelligence, and emotional capacity are not fixed traits, but qualities to be developed through effort, reflection, and learning. People with fixed mindsets react to setbacks with shame and retreat; they see mistakes as proof of inadequacy. Growth-minded people treat setbacks as data—feedback about what to improve. They understand that every downturn, every mistake, every moment of doubt is an opportunity to refine their approach and build their resilience. That perspective itself is an asset—they are more likely to persevere, adapt, and succeed.

Of course, none of this is free. It requires time, effort, and often money. It demands that you prioritize your own development above the siren call of instant gratification. It means saying no to quick wins—late nights of entertainment, impulse shopping, or endless scrolling—and yes to activities that yield returns only over months or years: a meditation practice, a habit of journaling, a commitment to weekly financial reviews, a regular exercise regimen, or a course to deepen your understanding of behavioral finance.

But the ROI on these investments is cumulative and compounding. Every moment you spend strengthening your emotional resilience, reinforcing your habits, or expanding your perspective makes the next financial decision—whether to save, spend, invest, or give—easier, clearer, and more aligned with your long-term goals. Over time, you become less reactive to market noise, less susceptible to comparison, more capable of patience, and more anchored in your values. Your financial life ceases to be a series of discrete wins and losses and transforms into a steady process of growth and alignment.

In this way, you become the CEO, CFO, and COO of your own life—responsible for managing your internal portfolio of skills, habits, and mindsets, no less than any external investments. And just as no competent executive would ignore half the assets under their control, you cannot afford to neglect the most important one: yourself.

So make a list of how you plan to invest in yourself this year. Choose one aspect—emotional resilience, habit formation, health, relationships, or mindset—and commit to a small daily practice. Track your progress. Reflect on how it affects your decisions. Then expand to the next area. Over time, you'll find that these self-directed investments create a multiplier effect, elevating every other strategy you pursue.

Because in the end, the markets will rise and fall. Strategies will shift. Products will come and go. But your ability to navigate all of it with wisdom and calm is the asset that truly endures.

You are the investment. And your behavior is the yield.

Emotional Resilience in Money Decisions

In the realm of personal finance, the most enduring advantage is not the highest return or the flashiest strategy, but the ability to withstand emotional turbulence and make sound decisions under pressure, and that ability—emotional resilience—is the hidden asset that separates fleeting winners from sustained achievers. When market headlines scream of crashes, when personal circumstances shift suddenly, when fear and greed ping-pong through your mind like relentless metronomes, it is resilience—the capacity to absorb shocks, recover quickly, and act with clarity rather than impulse—that determines whether you navigate the storm or let it capsize your progress.

Emotional resilience in money matters begins with the simple but profound realization that your feelings will inevitably sway your decisions if left unchecked. Pride might push you to chase a risk that feels exciting, only to burn you when it turns out to be reckless. Fear might drive you to panic-sell at a market low, locking in losses and forfeiting the recovery that follows. Envy might compel you to overspend to keep up, sabotaging the very security you claim to seek. These emotional impulses are neither moral failings nor character flaws—they are human by design. Our brains evolved to react swiftly to threats, rewards, and social cues. But in the modern financial arena, that ancient wiring often misfires, nudging us toward choices that feel urgent but are often detrimental.

Building emotional resilience requires acknowledging this reality and developing the tools to manage it. It starts with self-awareness: noticing, in real time, the subtle shifts in your mood as you watch your portfolio, check your bank balance, or scroll through social media. Do you feel a pang of jealousy when you see a peer's success? A twinge of regret over a purchase? A stab of anxiety about a looming bill? These feelings are neither good nor bad in themselves—they are data points, signals that something in your internal narrative is reacting to an external event.

The next step is to cultivate a pause—a mental buffer between the emotional signal and your response. This pause can be as simple as taking three deep breaths before making any financial decision, waiting 24 hours before reacting to a market dip, or consulting a written decision framework that reminds you of your long-term goals. In that brief space, the initial surge of emotion subsides enough for the rational mind to re-engage. You remind yourself: "Yes, the market is down, but my time horizon is 20 years." Or "I'm upset I didn't save more last month, but I can adjust moving forward." This practice of interrupting the knee-jerk reaction builds the muscle of resilience, allowing you to respond rather than react.

Journaling is another powerful tool. By recording not just the numbers, but your thoughts and feelings around financial events, you create a reflective practice that illuminates patterns in your emotional reactions. Perhaps you notice that you always feel panicked after reading a sensational headline, or that you are prone to overspending when stressed at work. These patterns, once identified, can be addressed systematically—through automation, by setting guardrails in your budget, or by scheduling deliberate "emotion check-ins" before making non-essential purchases.

Resilience also grows through exposure to mild stressors—in other words, by deliberately practicing under conditions that provoke manageable discomfort. Just as athletes build strength by lifting weights that challenge but don't injure them, emotionally resilient investors intentionally face small doses of financial discomfort. They might simulate a market crash by paper-trading through hypothetical downturns, or they might commit a small portion of their portfolio to a higher-risk asset to learn how they truly feel during volatility. By gaining firsthand experience of emotional reactions in controlled settings, you demystify your inner alarms and learn to navigate them more skillfully in real-life scenarios.

Community and accountability can further fortify emotional resilience. When you share your financial journey honestly with trusted peers or mentors—not just your victories, but your worries and mistakes— you gain perspective. You realize that everyone experiences fear and doubt. You learn strategies others have used to stay calm. You benefit from collective wisdom. And that sense of solidarity makes you less likely to feel isolated in your reactions, reducing the intensity of emotional impulses.

Importantly, emotional resilience is not about suppressing feelings. It's about acknowledging them without letting them dictate your decisions. It's feeling fear, and yet choosing to invest; feeling envy, and yet choosing generosity; feeling regret, and yet choosing forward momentum. It's recognizing that emotions are part of the human experience, but they are not reliable investment advisors.

Over time, as your resilience grows, you become less reactive to the market's mood swings and more anchored in your own. You stop confusing volatility for risk, because risk—defined by your personal goals and time horizon—remains constant even as markets gyrate. You learn that downturns are not geological catastrophes but opportunities for calm, measured action. You remain in the game, and that perseverance, more than any brilliant forecast, is what drives compounding returns.

Emotional resilience also extends beyond investing to every financial decision: the discipline to save before you spend, the steadiness to adhere to your budget in the face of temptation, the humility to ask for help when you're off-track, the courage to negotiate when you deserve more. In each case, the fork in the road is often marked by an emotion—excitement or fear, pride or shame—and resilience is the skill of choosing your values over your impulses.

Ultimately, the real return on investing in emotional resilience is not just measured in dollars, but in peace of mind. It's waking up without dread after a volatile session. It's sleeping soundly when your balance dips. It's making decisions from abundance rather than anxiety. And it's knowing that no matter what happens in the markets or in the economy, you have the internal resources to endure, adapt, and thrive.

That is the true power of resilience: not avoiding hardship, but becoming the person who is capable of meeting hardship with grace, learning from it, and emerging stronger on the other side. And in a world where uncertainty is the only certainty, that capacity is the most valuable asset you can own.

Thinking Long-Term in a Short-Term World

In the frenetic pace of modern life, where every moment is optimized for speed, where overnight success stories are celebrated more than sustained steady growth, and where social media algorithms reward the latest news cycle rather than enduring principles, the simple discipline of thinking long-term stands out as a profound act of countercultural defiance—and one that pays outsized dividends over a lifetime. To think long-term in a short-term world requires not only vision and patience, but also the behavioral infrastructure to resist the myriad forces pulling you toward immediate gratification, impulsive reaction, and the illusion of quick wins. It demands that you anchor yourself in a horizon that stretches decades into the future—even as every advertisement, notification, and headline screams for your immediate attention and action.

At its core, long-term thinking is the recognition that the most important outcomes—accumulated wealth, deep expertise, health, strong relationships, personal fulfillment—unfold not in days or months, but in years and decades. It is the willingness to sacrifice short-lived pleasures for enduring gains, to endure temporary discomfort for permanent progress, and to accept that some of the most transformative actions you can take today will only reveal their full impact far beyond the next quarterly report, annual review, or earnings call. Yet despite this understanding, few people build their decisions around multi-decade horizons, because our brains are wired to prioritize the proximal over the distal, the present over the possible.

This bias toward the short term can be devastating in financial life. When interest rates drop, the headlines scream about immediate market reactions. When a stock dips five percent in a day, panic spreads. When a new "hot" asset emerges, fear of missing out ignites. But the thoughtful investor—one who thinks long- term—sees these fluctuations not as determinants of fate, but as noise around a deeper trend. They resist the urge to act on every impulse, because they understand that wealth builds through consistency, not clarity. They understand that markets have survived wars, recessions, pandemics—and that over long spans, they have rewarded those who stayed the course.

Beyond investing, long-term thinking shapes how you view your career, your health, your relationships, and your habits. A job that offers a temporary spike in income may damage your health or steal years from your life. A diet that promises rapid results often proves unsustainable, leading to yo-yo cycles that undermine fitness. A relationship fueled by convenience rather than compatibility may feel thrilling at first, but it lacks the depth needed to endure. In each domain, the real returns come from choices that might feel boring, difficult, or insignificant in the moment—but which compound over time into something far greater than the sum of their parts.

The challenge, of course, is that thinking long-term requires a steady mind in a turbulent present. It demands that you build behavioral guardrails that protect you from the seductive siren call of immediacy. These guardrails might include automated savings and investing; lifetime frameworks for asset allocation that require minimal tinkering; principles for lifestyle inflation that slow spending growth even as income rises; monthly or quarterly rituals for reviewing goals rather than daily portfolio checks; and sober reminders of your personal mission that outweigh the noise of the latest trend. Without such structures, the temptation to deviate from even the best-laid long-term plans is immense—and often irresistible.

Moreover, long-term thinking is inherently a second-order skill. It means not only understanding the direct consequences of a decision, but also the downstream, compounding effects. When you decide to invest $500 today, you are not simply placing a bet on this week's returns—you are starting a process that, if maintained, will grow into something substantially larger over decades. When you choose to read or learn a new skill, you are not merely spending an hour—you are making an investment in your capacity to earn more, think differently, and solve complex problems far into the future. Recognizing these cascades of cause and consequence—rather than being blinded by the more immediate or sensational—sets you apart in a world entranced by instant gratification.

Crucially, thinking long-term also means preparing for uncertainty. Because while some outcomes can be anticipated—such as the power of compounding, the flow of career progression, or the benefits of healthy habits—others cannot. Policy changes, technological disruptions, global events can and will occur. Yet the person who thinks long-term builds robust systems designed not for perfect foresight, but for resilience: diversified portfolios, emergency funds, continuous learning, adaptable skill sets, and strong relationships that provide support in unexpected times. They don't chase precision; they chase robustness—knowing that in an unpredictable future, flexibility and durability are the most valuable assets.

Ultimately, long-term thinking is a mindset you cultivate through daily practice. It is choosing, in each moment, to prioritize the interests of your future self over the whims of your current self—to pay the small price of discipline today so you can enjoy the exponential benefits tomorrow. It is the quiet refusal to trade a lifetime of potential for the fleeting highs of a moment. And when sustained, it transforms not only your wealth, but your very experience of life: you move with steadiness in the face of fluctuation, with purpose beyond distraction, and with a sense of optimism grounded in the knowledge that real growth reserves its biggest returns for those patient enough to stay in the game.

Self-Awareness Over Strategy

In the grand labyrinth of financial advice, there exists an assumption so deeply held that few ever question it: that the right strategy—the perfect combination of asset allocation, exotic instruments, and market timing—holds the secret to success. Everywhere you look, experts debate the latest indicators, the most promising sectors, the algorithmic approaches. We believe that if we can only figure out the "strategy code," we will unlock a life of security, freedom, and prosperity. But there is a hidden truth beneath the surface of every financial plan and portfolio—it is not the grandeur of the strategy that ultimately determines your outcome, but the depth of your self-awareness. Because no matter how brilliant the blueprint, it is only as effective as the person who implements, adapts, and sustains it. And that person— inevitably fallible, emotional, and biased—must be known intimately for any strategy to work.

Self-awareness, in this context, is the practice of observing your own patterns—of thought, emotion, and behavior—as they relate to money decisions. It is noticing when you feel fear, greed, envy, or regret; it is recognizing the biases that cloud your judgment; it is understanding the triggers that lead you to stray from your plan. Most financial advice skips this step, assuming that rational actors can simply choose the right strategy and stick to it. But in practice, without self-awareness, we are all likely to fall prey to overconfidence, loss aversion, the herd instinct, or the siren call of shiny new opportunities. And when those impulses strike, the best-laid strategies become rubble.

To cultivate self-awareness, begin with your personal history with money. What messages did you internalize as a child—about scarcity, worth, achievement, or failure? How did your family talk about debt or success? Which early experiences shaped your sense of safety or dread around finances? These foundational beliefs, often unexamined, create a lens through which you interpret every financial event.

They color your perception of risk, your appetite for growth, and your tolerance for discomfort. By unearthing and naming these beliefs, you strip them of their unconscious power and can begin to develop healthier narratives.

Next, observe your real-time reactions to financial stimuli. Notice how you feel when a market headline alarms you. Note the twinge in your chest when you see a peer's new purchase. Pay attention to the impulse that arises when a sale email hits your inbox. Journaling these observations—recording not just what decision you made, but why you felt compelled to make it—creates a map of your emotional landscape. Over time, patterns emerge: maybe you overspend when you're stressed, or retract into safety when you feel underappreciated. These are not flaws. They are data. And data, once acknowledged, can be managed.

With that map in hand, you can design guardrails around your most vulnerable moments. If you know you're prone to panic-selling during a sharp market drop, automate a plan that keeps you invested. If you recognize that you splurge late at night, remove temptation by unsubscribing from promotional emails or setting a 24-hour rule. If you see that you chase novelty, build a rule that any new investment must pass a long-term checklist before getting a dime. These personalized guardrails leverage self-awareness to bolster any strategy, ensuring it survives the tests of emotion and environment.

Moreover, self-awareness fosters humility—a recognition that no strategy is infallible, and that every plan must be adjusted as circumstances and psychology evolve. Markets change. Taxes shift. Personal situations transform. But human nature remains stubbornly constant, prone to both brilliance and blind spots. By checking in with yourself regularly—through monthly reflections, quarterly reviews, or annual retreats— you maintain a dynamic relationship with your strategy. You ask: Is this still aligned with my goals? Am I following it out of habit, or because it still makes sense? Have I grown personally in ways that require new approaches? This level of conscious calibration keeps your strategy from calcifying into dogma.

Self-awareness also enhances learning from mistakes. When a trade goes wrong or an impulsive spend leaves you regretting, the self-aware individual does not simply blame the market or the consumer culture. They examine their own role: What bias led me astray? What emotional state was I in? How can I adjust my process to avoid repeating the mistake? This introspective cycle turns errors into breakthroughs, and setbacks into opportunities for growth.

Finally, self-awareness amplifies confidence. There is a special kind of peace that comes from knowing your own tendencies and having prepared for them. You no longer doubt every move or succumb to every impulse because you have tested yourself, faced your weaknesses, and built strategies to compensate. That inner steadiness allows you to engage with opportunities thoughtfully rather than reactively. It transforms strategy from a distant theory into a lived practice, because you carry it in your mind and heart, not just on a spreadsheet.

In the end, strategy without self-awareness is like a ship without a rudder—capable of speed, sure, but prone to drift, vulnerable to currents, and at constant risk of grounding. When you place self-awareness at the center of your financial life, every strategy becomes more robust, every decision more aligned, and every outcome more enduring. Because you don't just know what to do—you know *why* you do it, *how* you feel doing it, and *when* you need to course-correct. And that, more than any market insight, is the true asset that grows in value over a lifetime.

Your Financial Future Begins with Who You Are, Not What You Have

When we envision our financial futures, it is natural to picture numbers—account balances, portfolio values, projected returns. We imagine milestones: that balance in the bank, that net worth threshold, that luxury purchase or retirement lifestyle. Yet, as real as those figures may feel when we dream them, they are at best the *outcome* of a deeper process—and not the process itself. The real determinant of financial destiny is not the external assets you accumulate, but the internal qualities you cultivate. It begins with *who* you are—your habits, your mindsets, your character—and only then flows outward into the *what* you have. Recognizing this shifts the focus from chasing dollar signs to building your own capacity: the capacity to learn, adapt, persevere, and align every choice with a clear vision of your purpose and values.

Imagine two individuals with identical investment accounts, income levels, and liabilities. One approaches their finances as a series of external tasks: choosing funds, tracking numbers, responding to market swings. The other sees their financial life as an extension of their personal growth: each decision is an exercise in self-discipline, each setback an opportunity for learning, each goal a reflection of deeper aspirations.

When markets turn turbulent, the first person panics—their identity is tethered to the external balance, so every dip feels like a personal crisis. The second remains composed, because they understand that a portfolio is merely a reflection of behavior over time, and that setbacks are part of the process they have chosen to master. Over decades, their shared financial starting point diverges: the one who invested in internal strength compounds not just dollars, but wisdom, resilience, and peace of mind.

This dynamic underscores the central thesis: **your financial future is built not by the assets you hold, but by the person you become**. Numbers can rise and fall. They can be inherited, won, or lost. But the qualities you develop—self-awareness, emotional resilience, long-term orientation, consistent habits, contentment— remain with you no matter what the markets do. They are your most portable assets, your true currency in a world that will always change.

So how do you begin this inward journey toward financial character? It starts with **alignment**. Take a clear- eyed look at your deepest values and aspirations. What legacy do you want to leave? What problems do you want to solve? What kind of life do you want to lead, beyond the superficial trappings of success?

When your financial goals are rooted in these authentic desires, every savings plan, every budget line, and every investment decision becomes an act of self-expression rather than a checkbox on a to-do list.

Next, cultivate **self-discipline** through systems that automate good behavior. Automating savings, investments, and even charitable giving reduces the gap between intention and action, ensuring that your habits reinforce the person you want to be. As each small action repeats—every autopay, every direct deposit—you strengthen the neural pathways of discipline, making it easier to make aligned choices even when external pressures mount.

Then, develop **emotional mastery**. Recognize that uncertainty, volatility, and unexpected events are inevitable. Instead of fleeing in fear or chasing quick fixes, practice the art of pausing—breathing, reflecting, consulting your written principles—before reacting. This muscle of reflection transforms reactive impulses into considered responses and over time becomes the bedrock of composure in the face of market storms or personal financial challenges.

Equally important is a **long-term mindset**. Anchor your decisions in a horizon that extends decades, not days. This will mean resisting the siren calls of instant gratification—those shiny investments, those status- driven purchases, those get-rich-quick schemes—in favor of slow, incremental progress aligned with enduring goals. Remember that compound growth applies not just to money, but to habits: each day you show up for your future self builds upon the previous, until one day you look back and see a life fundamentally transformed.

Cultivate **self-awareness** by regularly reviewing not just your numbers, but your mental models. Keep a financial journal that records your decisions, the emotions you felt at the time, and the outcomes that followed. Over months and years, patterns will emerge—biases to correct, triggers to neutralize, strengths to leverage. This ongoing practice turns your inner landscape into a living dashboard, guiding your external strategy with ever-greater precision.

Finally, embrace **contentment and generosity** as pillars of your identity. Contentment frees you from the endless treadmill of comparison, allowing you to appreciate what you have while you build toward what you want. Generosity—whether in time, resources, or mentorship—expands your circle of well-being and creates a feedback loop of gratitude and purpose that no amount of accumulation alone can provide.

When these internal qualities become habitual, your financial future ceases to be a random walk of chance and market cycles. It becomes a deliberate creation, the natural expression of the person you have intentionally chosen to become. And that future, grounded in character, strong in resilience, and luminous with purpose, is the only one that truly endures.

So invest in yourself first. Build the behaviors, mindsets, and habits that will weather every storm, seize every opportunity, and align you with your deepest values. For in the end, what you have will always flow from who you are—and the most valuable asset you will ever own is the person you become along the way.

www.ingramcontent.com/pod-product-compliance
Lightning Source LLC
Chambersburg PA
CBHW051411070526
44584CB00023B/3382